Chile: the Other September 11

a book in the Radical History series

radical history

radical historY ☐

Also published in the Radical History series:

One Hundred Red Hot Years: *Big Moments of the 20th Century*

Politics on Trial: *Five Famous Trials of the 20th Century*

IWW: *A Wobbly Vision of the World*

The massive anticapitalist protest movements storming our globe prove that people have not surrendered to the lie of the "end of history" or submitted to the ever-deadening, ever-demoralizing capitalist status quo.

Radical History, an exciting new series from Ocean Press, challenges the attempt to separate human beings from their histories and communities and reflects a confidence in humanity's capacity to change our society and ourselves.

Radical History seeks to revive events, struggles and people erased from conventional (and conservative) media and memory, providing invaluable resources for a new generation of political activists.

The series will include eyewitness accounts and historic, forgotten or ignored documents. It will publish speeches and articles as well as new essays, chronologies and further resources. These books are edited and designed by young political activists.

Series Editor: Deborah Shnookal

"As long as someone controls your history the truth shall remain just a mystery."

–Ben Harper

Chile: the Other September 11

Edited by Pilar Aguilera and Ricardo Fredes

Ariel Dorfman

Salvador Allende

Joan Jara

Beatriz Allende

Pablo Neruda

Victor Jara

Fidel Castro

 Ocean Press
Melbourne ■ New York
www.oceanbooks.com.au

Cover Photo: Military Coup in Santiago de Chile, September 11, 1973. Pinochet's troops positioned on rooftop facing the Presidential Palace.

Cover design by Meaghan Barbuto

Copyright © 2003 Ocean Press

ISBN 1-876175-50-8

First printed 2003

Printed in Australia

Library of Congress Control Number 2002107118

Published by Ocean Press
Australia GPO Box 3279 Melbourne, Victoria 3001, Australia
Tel 61 3 9326 4280
Fax 61 3 9329 5040
email: info@oceanbooks.com.au

USA PO Box 1186 Old Chelsea Station, New York, NY 10113-1186, USA
Tel 718 246 4160

Ocean Press Distributors
United States and Canada
Consortium
1045 Westgate Drive, Suite 90
Saint Paul, MN 55114-1065
1-800-283-3572

Britain and Europe
Global Book Marketing
38 King Street, London WC2E 8JT, UK
orders@globalbookmarketing.co.uk

Australia and New Zealand
Astam Books
57-61 John Street, Leichhardt, NSW 2040, Australia
info@astambooks.com.au

Cuba and Latin America
Ocean Press
Calle 21 #406, Vedado, Havana, Cuba

www.oceanbooks.com.au

Contents

"Llegó volando el
cuervo sobre mi suelo
Para sembrar las ruina
y el desconsuelo."

–Patricio Manns

Introduction

Pilar Aguilera and Ricardo Fredes

On September 11, 1973, we awoke to a country in turmoil. What many people had predicted was actually happening: the armed forces of Chile were staging a coup d'état to overthrow democratically elected President Salvador Allende. We heard that the Moneda Presidential Palace was being bombed, but very little information was broadcast over the radio; instead there were mainly military communiqués and military marches being played.

On the evening of September 13, a group of soldiers, led by a captain, came to our home and proceeded to search for weapons. When they didn't find any, they took my father away with them. They also took our books about socialism or left politics, and we found out afterward that such books had been burned. About an hour later they returned for my older brother and he was taken, beaten up and brought back to us. The captain said to my mother, "Here's your son – we brought him back so he can work for you, because we executed your husband."

About two months later, a gaunt man walked into Ricardo Fredes' home. No one recognized him at first. Hector "Tito" Fredes, Ricardo's father, had been held in one of the many concentration camps set up by the military. For many, such experiences marked the beginning of a long period of suffering, torture, anxiety and exile, part of the darkest chapter in Chilean history.

> When they speak of the bombing of La Moneda Palace...
> you should know that this act is the equivalent of bombing
> the New York Public Library at 42nd Street and Fifth
> Avenue during the work day.

This was how, one year after the coup, José Yglesias tried to
explain to U.S. citizens the impact of the terror experienced by
ordinary Chileans that day in 1973. The idea of an "other"
September 11 must seem incredible to some. But when Chileans
saw the photos of New Yorkers holding up images of missing
loved ones after the September 11 attacks, the scene was fright-
eningly familiar, and as Ariel Dorfman commented: "During the
last 28 years, September 11 has been a date of mourning, for me
and millions of others."

This book reclaims September 11, not only for the sake of
history but also for the thousands of dreams that were shattered on
the morning of September 11, 1973, and for those for whom, as
Dorfman recalled, "the world [would] never be the same again."
The horror, confusion and seemingly endless terror in both cases
are poignant. In Chile the nightmare continued for 17 years, and
as one young Chilean remarked a year after the coup, "It took me
a long time to realize that what was happening was for real and not
a nightmare."

Ariel Dorfman powerfully links the two September 11s, and
provides a backdrop for the rest of the pieces contained in this
book. Pablo Neruda, whose poetry has often been stripped of its politics by the mainstream, demands judgment of "those hands stained
by the dead he killed with his terror," in his poem from "A Call for
the Destruction of Nixon and Praise for the Chilean Revolution."

The intensity of the writings included in this book are an
evocative and timely reminder that the horror visited upon the
Chilean people was largely the result of continuous U.S. involvement in our country, which climaxed during the years of Salvador
Allende's Popular Unity government (1970-73). James Cockcroft's
chronology alone should serve as a damning indictment of U.S.
and CIA involvement in Chile from the 1960s right up to the coup.
Also included in this book is Fidel Castro's speech just days after

the coup, which provides an uncompromising and powerful political analysis of events leading up to the coup.

This book also gives a voice to those who, from the very beginning, claimed the fascist nature of the Chilean and U.S. forces eventually involved in the coup. Victor Jara, the well-known Chilean composer and singer, wrote these lines while under detention in the infamous National Stadium where he was brutally executed:

> *What horror the face of fascism creates!*
> *They carry out their plans with knife-like precision.*
> *Nothing matters to them.*
> *To them, blood equals medals,*
> *Slaughter is an act of heroism…*
> *How hard it is to sing when I must sing of horror.*
> *Horror which I am living,*
> *Horror which I am dying.*

The "knife-like precision" of the coup could not have happened without funding and advice from the United States. Contemplating the prospect of Allende's electoral victory in 1970, Secretary of State Henry Kissinger spoke plainly: "I don't see why we need to stand by and watch a country go communist because of the irresponsibility of its own people."

When Allende assumed office, more than 100 U.S. corporations had established themselves in Chile. Among these were some of the top U.S.-based multinational corporations. These included the major car manufacturers, oil companies, Dow and DuPont chemicals and International Telephone and Telegraph (ITT) among others. Their collective investment in Chile was nearly $1 billion, with ITT's investment ranking the highest, at $200 million, according to *Business Week*, April 10, 1971.

The election of the Allende government was followed by an extensive CIA-initiated destabilization campaign. Washington could not and would not "stand by" and let a Latin American country determine its own fate. A country that had chosen a "peaceful road to socialism" would not be tolerated. As Allende astutely pointed out: "Foreign capital and imperialism, united with reactionary elements, created the climate for the armed forces to break with their tradition [of respecting constitutional guarantees]."

For Chileans all over the world September 11, 2001, meant reliving the horror they had experienced in Chile and feeling again the loss, not only for loved ones but also the loss of hope, and a sense that the nightmare had just begun. Chileans had dared to want to determine their own future, create their own society. Instead, Chile was for decades plunged into a darkness from which it has not recovered. The repercussions of the coup are still felt today; and Chile, generally speaking, has not confronted its past. After 1973, Pinochet tried to erase the past so that young Chileans were kept ignorant of their country's history. Patricio Guzmán's 1997 documentary, "Obstinate Memory," shows Chilean university students confronted *for the first time* with images of the September 11 military attacks on the Presidential Palace. Face to face with their suppressed history, the students break down in anger and disbelief.

There are those who do not want to relive the horror, and those who choose to remain indifferent, and those who choose to forget. But we must face the past, learn from it and seek the truth. It is time now to "overcome [that] gray and bitter moment where treason [tried] to impose itself," and live out Allende's dream so eloquently articulated in his last radio address to the people of Chile: "History is ours, and the people will make it."

"What does a person do at that moment? When two hours before, everything was as it always had bee and then all at once you see this heavy artillery, and all these planes flying over La Moneda, the whole horrible sequence of events."

–Ana María, young Chilean activist, 1973

The Last September 11
Ariel Dorfman

I have been through this before.

During the last 28 years, Tuesday, September 11 has been a date of mourning, for me and millions of others, ever since that day in 1973 when Chile lost its democracy in a military coup, that day when death irrevocably entered our lives and changed us forever. And now, almost three decades later, the malignant gods of random history have wanted to impose upon another country that dreadful date, again a Tuesday, once again an 11th of September filled with death.

The differences and distances that separate the Chilean date from the American are, one must admit, considerable. The depraved terrorist attack against the most powerful nation on Earth has and will have consequences which affect all humanity. It is possible that it may constitute, as President Bush has stated, the start of World War III and it is probable that it will be branded in the manuals of the future as the day when the planet's history shifted forever. Whereas very few of the eight billion people alive today could remember or would be able to identify what happened in Chile.

And yet, from the moment when, transfigured, I watched on our television screen here in North Carolina that second plane exploding into the World Trade Center's South Tower, I have been haunted by the need to understand and extract the hidden meaning of the juxtaposition and coincidence of these two September 11s – which in my case becomes even more enigmatic and personal because it is a violation that conjoins the two foundational cities of my existence, the New York which gave me refuge and joy during 10 years of my infancy and the Santiago which protected my adolescence under its mountains and made me into a man, the two cities that offered me my two languages, English and Spanish. It has been, therefore, tentatively, breathing slowly to overcome the emotional shock; making every effort not to look again and again at the contaminating photo of the man who falls vertically, so straight, so straight, from the heights of that building; trying to stop thinking about the last seconds of those plane passengers who know that their imminent doom will also kill thousands of their own innocent compatriots; in the midst of frantic phone calls that should tell me if my friends in Manhattan are well and that nobody answers; it is in the middle of all this turmoil that I yield myself to the gradual realization that there is something horribly familiar, even recognizable, in this experience that (North) Americans are now passing through.

The resemblance I am evoking goes well beyond a facile and superficial comparison – for instance, that both in Chile in 1973 and in the States today, terror descended from the sky to destroy the symbols of national identity, the Presidential Palace in Santiago, the icons of financial and military power in New York and Washington. No, what I recognize is something deeper, a parallel suffering, a similar pain, a commensurate disorientation, echoing what we lived through in Chile as of that September 11. Its most extraordinary incarnation – I still cannot believe what I am witnessing – is that on the screen I see hundreds of relatives wandering the streets of New York, clutching the photos of their sons, fathers, wives, lovers, daughters, begging for information, asking if they are alive or dead, the whole United States forced to look into the abyss of what it means to be *desaparecido*, with no certainty or funeral possible for those beloved men and women who are missing. And I also recognize and repeat that sensation of extreme unreality that invariably accompanies great disasters caused by human iniquity, so much more difficult to cope with than natural catastrophes. Over and over again I hear phrases that remind me of what people like me would mutter to themselves during the 1973 military coup and the days that followed: "This cannot be happening to us. This sort of excessive violence happens to other people and not to us, we have only known this form of destruction through movies and books and remote photographs. If it's a nightmare, why can't we awaken from it?" And words reiterated unceasingly, 28 years ago and now again in the year 2001: "We have lost our innocence. The world will never be the same."

What has come to an explosive conclusion, of course, is the United States' famous exceptionalism, that attitude which allowed the citizens of this country to imagine themselves as beyond the sorrows and calamities that have plagued less fortunate peoples around the world. None of the great battles of the 20th century had touched the continental United States. Even the Pearl Harbor "Day of Infamy" which is being tiredly extricated from the past as the only possible analogous incident, occurred thousands of miles away. It is that complacent invulnerability which has been fractured forever. Life in these United States will have to share, from now on, the precariousness and uncertainty that is the daily lot of the enormous majority of this planet's other inhabitants.

In spite of the tremendous pain, the intolerable losses that this apocalyptic crime has visited upon the American public, I wonder if this trial does not constitute one of those opportunities for regeneration and self-knowledge that, from time to time, is given to certain nations. A crisis of this magnitude can lead to renewal or destruction, it can be used for good or for evil, for peace or for war, for aggression or for reconciliation, for vengeance or for justice, for the militarization of a society or its humanization. One of the ways for Americans to overcome their trauma and survive the fear and continue to live and thrive in the midst of the insecurity which has suddenly swallowed them is to admit that their suffering is neither unique nor exclusive, that they are connected, as long as they are willing to look at themselves in the vast mirror of our common humanity, with so many other human beings who, in apparently faraway zones, have suffered similar situations of unanticipated and often protracted injury and fury.

Could this be the hidden and hardly conceivable reason destiny has decided that the first contemporary attack on the essence and core of the United States, would transpire precisely on the very anniversary that commemorates the military takeover in Chile; a takeover that a government in Washington nourished and sustained in the name of the American people? Could it be a way to mark the immense challenge that awaits the citizens of this country, particularly its young, now that they know what it really means to be victimized, now that they can grasp the sort of collective hell survivors withstand when their loved ones have disappeared without a body to bury, now that they have been given the chance to draw closer to and comprehend the multiple variations of the many September 11s that are scattered throughout the globe, the kindred sufferings that so many peoples and countries endure?

The terrorists have wanted to single out and isolate the United States as a satanic state. The rest of the planet, including many nations and men and women who have been the object of American arrogance and intervention reject – as I categorically do – this demonization. It is enough to see the almost unanimous outpouring of grief from most of the world, the offers of help, the expressions of solidarity, the determination to claim the dead of this mass murder as our dead.

It remains to be seen if this compassion shown to the mightiest power on this planet will be reciprocated. It is still not clear if the United States – a country formed in great measure by those who have themselves escaped vast catastrophes, famines, dictatorships, persecution – if the men and women of this nation, so full of hope and tolerance, will be able to feel that same empathy toward the other outcast members of our species. We will find out in the days and years to come if the new Americans, forged in pain and resurrection, are ready and open and willing to participate in the arduous process of repairing our shared, damaged humanity. Creating, all of us together, a world in which we never again lament another, terrifying September 11.

March 25, 1970

A meeting of the White House "Committee of 40," headed by Henry Kissinger and in charge of U.S. plans to prevent Allende's ascendancy to the presidency or, failing that, to destabilize his regime until a military coup can overthrow him, approves $125,000 for a "spoiling operation" in Chile.

I Begin by Invoking Walt Whitman

Pablo Neruda

Pablo Neruda, winner of the Nobel Prize for Literature in 1971, is Chile's most famous poet and his poetry is loved throughout the world. He died in Santiago de Chile on September 23, 1973, just days after the coup.

Because I love my country
I claim you, essential brother,
old Walt Whitman with your gray hands,

so that, with your special help
line by line, we will tear out by the roots
this bloodthirsty President Nixon.

There can be no happy man on earth,
no one can work well on this planet
while that nose continues to breathe in Washington.

Asking the old bard to confer with me
I assume the duties of a poet
armed with a terrorist's sonnet

because I must carry out with no regrets
this sentence, never before witnessed,
of shooting a criminal under siege,

who in spite of his trips to the moon
has killed so many here on earth
that the paper flies up and the pen is unsheathed

to set down the name of this villain
who practices genocide from the White House.

Last Words Transmitted by Radio Magallanes, September 11, 1973

Salvador Allende

It is Chile's darkest hour, one that Allende prophetically says will bring down "infamy" on the heads of "those who have violated their commitments." Inside La Moneda, the Presidential Palace, Allende and a handful of followers defend themselves with bazookas and machine guns, repeatedly refusing to surrender. The 65-year-old president uses a palace hookup with a radio station to address the Chilean people one last time before bombers force the station off the air. In what he calls "this gray and bitter moment," Allende persists in his "faith in Chile and its destiny." The "calm metal" of his voice intones to Chile's workers: "Much sooner than later the great avenues through which free men walk to build a better society will open." Allende's press secretary Frida Modak later recalls: "I shall never forget the last time I saw Allende, his head covered by a helmet, his hand holding the machine gun."

I will pay with my life defending the principles that are so dear to this homeland. Infamy will descend upon those who have violated their commitments, have failed to live up to their word, have broken the doctrine of the armed forces.

The people must be alert and vigilant. You must not let yourselves be provoked, not let yourselves be massacred, but you must also defend your conquests. You must defend the right to construct, through your own effort, a dignified and better life.

A word for those who, calling themselves democrats, have been instigating this uprising; for those who, saying they are representatives of the people, have been confused and acting stupidly to make possible this step that flings Chile down a precipice.

In the name of the most sacred interests of the people, in the name of the homeland, I call to you to tell you to keep faith. Neither criminality nor repression can hold back history. This stage will be surpassed; it is a hard and difficult moment.

It is possible they will smash us, but tomorrow belongs to the people, the workers. Humanity advances toward the conquest of a better life.

Compatriots: It is possible that they will silence the radios, and I will take my leave of you. In these moments the planes are flying overhead. They may riddle us with bullets. But know that we are here, at least with this example, to show that in this country there are people who know how to meet their obligations. I will do so, as commanded by the people and by my own conscientious will, that of a president who bears the dignity of his charge... [interruption]

Perhaps this is my last opportunity to address myself to you. The air force has bombed the towers of Radio Portales and Radio Corporación. My words are not tainted by bitterness, but rather by deception. I hope there may be a moral punishment for those who have betrayed the oath they took as soldiers of Chile... Admiral Merino, who has designated himself commander of the navy; Mr. Mendoza, the callous general who only yesterday declared his loyalty to the government, and has been named director general of the *Carabineros* [Chilean national police].

In the face of these facts, the only thing left for me to say to the workers is: I will not resign! I say to you that I am sure that the seed that we now plant in the dignified conscience of thousands and thousands of Chileans cannot be definitively buried.

They have the power, they can smash us, but social processes are not detained, not through crimes or power. History is ours, and the people will make it.

Workers of my country, I want to thank you for the loyalty which you have always shown, the trust which you placed in a man who was only the interpreter of the great desires for justice, who gave his word that he would respect the constitution and the law, and I did just so.

In this moment of definition, the last thing I can say to you is that I hope you will learn this lesson: Foreign capital and imperialism, united with reactionary elements, created the climate for the armed forces to break with their tradition [of respecting constitutional guarantees]. General Schneider and Commander Araya, who belong to that tradition, are now victims of the same social sectors that right now are in their homes, waiting to take power to continue defending their huge estates and privileges.

I address myself above all to the modest women of our country, to the peasant woman who believed in us, to the working woman who worked harder, to the mother who knew of our concern for her children. I address myself to the patriotic professionals of our land, to those professionals who were working against the sedition carried out by the professional, class-ridden schools that defend the advantages capitalist society gives them.

I address myself to the youth, to those who sang, who gave their joy and spirit to the struggle. I address myself to the Chilean man: to the worker, the peasant, the intellectual, to those who will be persecuted by the fascism that has been present in our country for many hours now. Those terrorists who have been blowing up bridges, cutting railway lines, destroying oil and gas pipelines – in the face of the silence of those who have had the obligation to raise their voices – history will judge them.

Radio Magallanes will surely soon be silenced, and the calm metal of my voice will no longer reach you. It does not matter. You shall continue to hear me. I shall always be at your side, and you will remember me at least as a dignified man who was loyal to his country.

The people must defend themselves, but not sacrifice themselves. The people must not let themselves be leveled or mowed down, but neither can they let themselves be humiliated.

Workers of my homeland! I have faith in Chile and its destiny. Other people will overcome this gray and bitter moment where treason tries to impose itself. May you continue to know that much sooner than later the great avenues through which free men walk to build a better society will open.

Long live Chile! Long live the people! Long live the workers! These are my last words. I am sure that my sacrifice will not be in vain; I am sure that it will at least be a moral lesson which will punish felony, cowardice and treason.

"I don't see why we need to stand by and watch a country go communist due to the irresponsibility of its own people."

–Henry Kissinger

To Chile, To Allende

A. Appercelle

The sun
the bloodying
sea
cameras
      snap –
The water is transparent
white between our fingers
      it flows
"El Fascismo-el Fascismo"
– Take your guitar
             Chilean
and play   play
until our arteries burst
don't let the dust
swallow your brain
Strike!
      the women
will give birth to grenades.

Translated from the French by Serge Gavronsky

Poem Delivered Before an Assembly of Colored People...

Ishmael Reed
an extract

President Waterbugger only your crimes
Want to be near you now
Your daughters have moved out of town
Your wife refuses to hold your hand
On the elevator
Inexplicably, Lincoln's picture
Just fell from the wall
Next time you kill a poet
You'd better read his poems first
Or they will rise up and surround you
Like 1945 fire cannons a few miles from
Berlin
And History will find no trace of
Your ashes in the bunker of your hell

The Coup
Joan Jara

Joan Jara was a well-known dancer and choreographer from Britain. She is the widow of Victor Jara and in the following piece she vividly recounts the events that unfolded around her on the day of the coup.

September 11, 1973

I wake early as usual. Victor is still asleep, so I get out of bed quietly and wake Manuela who has to get to school early... We have breakfast, Manuela and I, and set out for school. It isn't far by car, but difficult to reach by public transport even if there were any. Luckily we still have some petrol. We are obviously the only people stirring. Everyone else seems to have decided to stay in bed, except of course the maids, who get up early and go to queue for bread at the bakery on the corner. Monica had come back with the news that Allende's car had already raced down Avenida Colón, accompanied by its usual escort, much earlier than usual. People in the bread queue and in the newspaper kiosk were saying that something was afoot.

Manuel de Salas is full of students. There is no sign of the strike here. Only a tiny percentage of families are not supporters of Popular Unity. On the way home I switch on the car radio and the news comes through that Valparaíso has been sealed off and that unusual troop movements are taking place. The trade unions are calling for all workers to assemble in their places of work, because this is an emergency, a red alert.

I hurry home to tell Victor. He is already up when I arrive and is fiddling with the transistor radio trying to get Magallanes or one of the other radio stations that support Popular Unity. "This seems to be it," we say to each other, "it has really started."

Victor was due that morning to sing at the Technical University, for the opening of a special exhibition about the horrors of civil war and fascism, where Allende was going to speak. "Well, that won't happen," I said. "No, but I think I should go anyway, while you go and fetch Manuela from school – because it's better that you're all at home together – I'll make some phone calls to try to find out what is happening."

As I drove out of the courtyard again, our neighbors were beginning to gather. They were talking loudly and excitedly, already beginning to celebrate. I passed them without glancing at them, but looking back in the mirror, I saw one of the "ladies" squat down and give the most obscene gesture in Chilean sign language to my receding back.

Back at the school, I found that instructions had been given for the younger students to go home, while the teachers and older students were to stay behind. I collected Manuela and, on the way home, although the reception was bad, we heard Allende on the radio. It was reassuring to hear his voice from the Moneda Palace... but it sounded almost like a speech of farewell.

I found Victor in the studio listening to the radio and together we heard the confusion as almost all the Popular Unity stations went off the air when their aerials were bombed or they were taken over by the military, and martial music replaced Allende's voice...

> This is the last time I shall be able to speak to you... I shall not resign... I will repay with my life the loyalty of the people... I say to you: I am certain that the seeds we have sown in the conscience of thousands and thousands of Chileans cannot be completely eradicated... neither crime nor force are strong enough to hold back the process of social change. History belongs to us, because it is made by the people...

It was the speech of a heroic man who knew he was about to die, but at that moment we heard it only in snatches. Victor was called to the phone in the middle... I could hardly bear to listen to it.

Victor had been waiting for me to come back in order to go out. He had decided that he had to go to his place of work, the Technical University, obeying the instructions of the workers' confederation (CUT). Silently he poured our last can of petrol, reserved for emergencies like this, into the car and as he did so, I saw one of our neighbors, a pilot of the National Airline, look over the balcony of his house and shout something mocking at Victor, who replied with a smile.

It was impossible to say goodbye properly. If we had done so I should have held on to him and never let him go, so we were casual. "Mamita, I'll be back as soon as I can... you know I have to go... just be calm." "Chao..." and when I looked again, Victor had gone.

Listening to the radio, between one military march and another, I heard the announcements. "*Bando Numero Uno... Bando Numero Dos...*" military orders announcing that Allende had been given an ultimatum to surrender by the commanders of the armed forces, led by General Augusto Pinochet... that unless he surrender by midday the Moneda Palace would be bombed...

The girls were playing in the garden, when suddenly there was the thunder and whine of a diving jet plane and then a tremendous explosion. It was like being in the war again... I rushed out to bring the children indoors, closed the wooden shutters and convinced them that it was all a game. But the jets kept on diving and it seemed that the rockets they were firing were falling on the *población* (shanty-town) just above us toward the mountains. I think it was at this moment that any illusions I may have had died in me... if this was what we were up against, what hope could there be?

Then came the helicopters, low over the treetops of the garden. From the balcony of our bedroom I saw them, hovering like sinister insects, raking Allende's house with machine gun fire. High above, toward the cordillera, another plane circled. We could hear the high whine of its engine for hours on end – the control plane, perhaps?

Soon after, the telephone rings. I rush to answer it and hear

Victor's voice, "Mamita, how are you? I couldn't get to the phone before... I'm here in the Technical University... You know what's happening, don't you?" I tell him about the dive bombers, but that we are all well. "When are you coming home?" "I'll ring you later on... the phone is needed now... chao."

Then there is nothing to do but listen to the radio, to the military pronouncements between one march and another. The neighbors are outside in the patio, talking excitedly, some are standing on their balconies to get a better view of the attack on Allende's house... they are bringing out the drinks... one house has even put out a flag.

We listen to the news of the Moneda Palace being bombed and set on fire... we wonder if Allende has survived... there is no announcement about it. A curfew is being imposed. Quena rings to know how we are and I tell her that Victor isn't here, that he has gone to the university. "Oh, my God!" she exclaims, and rings off.

We have to assume now that all the telephones are tapped, but Victor rings about 4:30 p.m. "I have to stay here... it will be difficult to get back because of the curfew. I'll come home, first thing in the morning when the curfew is lifted... Mamita, I love you." "I love you too," but I choke as I say it and he has already hung up.

I did go to bed that night, but of course I couldn't sleep. All around the neighborhood in the darkness you could hear sudden bursts of gunfire. I waited for morning wondering if Victor was cold, if he could sleep, wherever he was, wishing that he had taken at least a jacket with him, wondering if, as the curfew had been suddenly postponed until later in the evening, perhaps he had left the university and gone to someone's house nearby.

It was late next morning before the curfew was lifted and the maids trooped out to buy bread at the corner shop. But today the queue was controlled by soldiers who butted people with their guns and threatened them. I longed for Victor to come home, to hear the hum of the car as it drew up under the wisteria. I calculated how long it ought to take him to make the journey from the university... As I waited, I realized that there was no money in the house, so I set out to walk the couple of blocks to the little shop belonging to Alberto who might be able to change a check for me.

On my way, two trucks zoomed past me. They were packed with civilians armed with rifles and machine guns. I realized that they were our local fascists coming out of their holes into the light of day.

Alberto was very scared, and with reason. In the preceding weeks a couple of bombs had already exploded outside his shop. But he was good enough to change a check for me and asked after Victor. I hurried home, and on my way, bumped into a friend, the wife of one of the members of Inti-Illimani [Chilean folk-music group] who lived nearby. She was in a state of shock too, and all alone, because Inti was in Europe. By mutual consent she came home with me and didn't leave until several days later. She had been ill the previous day and had not gone to the government department where she worked. Now she was in agony, thinking about what might have happened there and how her colleagues had fared.

Together now we waited, but Victor didn't come. Glued to the television, although near to vomiting with what I saw, seeing the faces of the generals talking about "eradicating the cancer of Marxism" from the country; hearing the official announcement that Allende was dead; seeing the film of the ruins of the Moneda Palace and of Allende's home, endlessly repeated, with shots of his bedroom, his bathroom – or what remained of them – with an "arsenal of weapons" that seemed pathetically small considering his detectives had to protect him against terrorist attacks. It was only late in the afternoon that I heard that the Technical University had been *reducida* (captured) – that tanks had entered the university precincts in the morning and that a large number of "extremists" had been arrested.

My lifeline, although a dubious one because it had ears, was the telephone. I knew that Quena was trying to find out what had happened to Victor. She, better than I, could try to find out discreetly. I was afraid to act, afraid of identifying Victor before the military authorities. I didn't want to draw attention to him... perhaps anyway he had managed to get out of the university before it was attacked... that was my hope.

Wednesday night passed, another cold night, bitterly cold for September. The bed was large and empty and there was an agonising vacuum at my side. I slept fitfully and dreamt Victor's touch, his warm limbs entwined with mine. I woke to empty darkness and in an agony of fear for him... I remembered his nightmares.

Next morning, still no news. I tried to phone different people who might know what had happened in the Technical University. Nobody was sure about anything... then Quena again – she had found out that the detainees from the university had been taken to Estadio Chile, the big boxing stadium where Victor had sung so often and where the Song Festivals had taken place. She wasn't sure if Victor had been among them; the women – most of them had been released and had given her the news... only they weren't absolutely sure that Victor had been arrested with the rest because they had been separated from the men.

In the afternoon the phone rang. Heart jumping, I ran to answer it. An unknown voice, very nervous, asked for *compañera* Joan... "Yes, yes," then there was a message for me: "*Compañera*, you don't know me, but I have a message for you from you husband. I've just been released from the Estadio Chile... Victor is there... he asked me to tell you that you should be calm and stay in the house with the children... that he left the car outside the Technical University in the car park, if maybe, someone can fetch it for you... he doesn't think that he will be released from the stadium."

"*Compañero*, thank you for ringing me, but what did he mean by that?"

"That is what he told me to tell you. Good luck, *compañera*!" and he hung up.

When Quena rang a few minutes later, I gave her the news. She began to do everything she could to find out more, to find out what would be the best way of trying to get Victor out. She even went to see Cardinal Silva Henriquez, asking him to intervene. What immobilised me was the fear of identifying Victor, if they had not already done so; his own instructions to me, which I assumed were for the best and my blind faith in the power and organization of the Communist Party which would, I thought, know the best way of saving people like Victor.

Even now, at this stage, I had no real idea of the horrors that were taking place. We were deprived of news and information, although rumors were rife. A responsible political leader phoned me to tell me that General Prats (Popular Unity) was advancing from the north with an army... this must be the beginning of the civil war about which we had been warned. (Only later did we learn that General Prats had been imprisoned and that, during the night of September 10, even before the coup really began, there had been a purge of all officers suspected of supporting Allende's government.)

During the short time the curfew was lifted on Friday, I decided to make the journey across Santiago to fetch the car. I thought we ought to have it in case it was necessary to leave home in a hurry. It was my first excursion outside our neighborhood and in the midday sun everything looked unnaturally normal: the buses were running again, there was food in the shops. The only abnormality was the number of soldiers in the streets, at every corner, but there were plenty of people about, walking hurriedly, their faces emptied of expression. As the bus made its slow way along the Alameda, we passed the Moneda Palace – or rather the shell of it, roped off from the square. Many people were passing up and down in front of it, I suppose with curiosity to see the results of the bombing and the fire, but no one showed any feelings at all, either of rage and sadness or of satisfaction.

Central Station and the stalls outside were as busy as ever. I got off the bus and hesitated on the corner of the side road leading to the Estadio Chile. I stood looking at the crowd of people outside, the guards with their machine guns at the ready. It was impossible to get near it, but anyway, what could I do? I walked the few blocks to the Technical University... the campus and the new modern building were strangely deserted...

And then I realize that the great plate-glass windows and doors are all broken, the façade of the building damaged and bullet scarred. The car park in front, usually full to overflowing, is empty except for our little car looking solitary in the middle of it. There must be military guards about, but I don't notice them. I see only an old man sitting on a wall some distance away. I put one foot in front of the other until I reach the car, fumbling for my keys, and I find that I am stepping in a pool of blood which is seeping from under the car... that where there should be a window there is nothing... the car is full of broken glass. I think, "This can't be ours" and begin to try the keys to see if they fit. Then I see that the old man is walking toward me. "Who are you?" he shouts at me. "This is my car," I stutter at him. "This is my husband's car. He left it here." "That's all right then," the old man says. "I was looking after it for Don Victor. Look, I found his identity card on the ground. You'd better have it," and he passes it to me.

"But where did all the blood come from, whose blood is it?" I ask.

"Oh, I expect someone knifed a thief who was trying to steal it. A lot of blood has been spilt around here lately. You'd better go as quickly as you can. It's not safe." And he helps me clean the broken glass from the car seat so that I can drive it and sees me on my way.

That was Friday. I don't know how I got through Saturday. People phoned me. I phoned people. Marta came to see me. Angel had been arrested and taken to the National Stadium. Bad news of other friends came to me. The Popular Unity leaders were all detained or in hiding, being hunted like criminals. Other friends had disappeared.

As I lay down on the bed on Saturday night – I can't say to sleep – staring at the ceiling through the long hours of the night, a different sort of cold hopelessness began to seep over me. Suddenly, with my heart thudding, I sat up abruptly. Victor wasn't there.

As soon as it was light I went to the wardrobe and began to get out clothes which I had not used for ages... respectable, Marks & Spencer clothes, which would make me look like a foreigner. I put my hair up, put dark glasses on and tried to steel myself to go to the British Embassy to ask them to help Victor. It was too early, of course. I had to wait for the curfew to end. As it was Sunday, I had to find the ambassador's residence, rather than go to the embassy itself in the center. It was one of those large mansions of the *barrio alto* with high wrought-iron gates and railings, closed and with a police guard outside. No sign of life. I rang the bell and waited until one of the servants came out. "I am a British subject. I need help."

I thought that he would open the gate, but no. He told me to wait. I waited. The police outside were looking me over. I wondered if I looked British enough. Then the main door of the mansion opened and a very obviously British young man approached the gates. "Oh, sorry about all this cloak and dagger stuff. Orders from above, you know. What can I do for you?"

I told him in incoherent and stuttering English, which wouldn't come out properly, that my husband was in the Estadio Chile, that I feared desperately for his safety and could they help me. Peering at me through the firmly locked gates, he said, "Oh, but is he a British subject? You know we can't do anything if he is not British." "No, he's Chilean, but I fear that he may be in special danger, because he is a well-known person. Please see if you can do anything to get him out... if they know that the British Embassy is concerned about him, perhaps it will be better."

"Well, I don't think that there is very much we can do, but under the circumstances, perhaps the most appropriate thing would be for our naval attaché to make enquiries about him with the military authorities. I'll see what we can do... I can't promise anything. I'll ring you if I have any news."

So I came home, wondering if I had done the right thing, hoping that I hadn't betrayed Victor. If he had thrown away his identity card it was because he hoped he wouldn't be recognized. *Unless he was already dead.*

Monday is a blank. I suppose I went through the motions of being alive. By military decree we must put the flags out tomorrow, to celebrate Chile's Independence Day, *Fiestas Patrias.*

Tuesday, September 18
About an hour after the curfew is lifted, I hear the noise of the gate being rattled, as though someone is trying to get in. It is still locked... I look out of the bathroom window and see a young man standing outside. He looks harmless, so I go down. He says to me very quietly. "I am looking for the *compañera* of Victor Jara. Is this the house? Please trust me – I am a friend," and he brings out his identity card to show me. "May I come in for a minute? I need to talk to you." He looks nervous and worried. He whispers, "I am a member of the Communist Youth."

I open the gate to let him in and we sit down in the living room opposite each other. "I'm sorry, I had to come and find you... I'm afraid I have to tell you that Victor is dead... his body has been found in the morgue. He was recognized by one of the *compañeros* working there. Please, be brave, you must come with me to see if it is him... was he wearing dark-blue underpants? You must come, because his body has already been there almost 48 hours and unless it is claimed they will take him away and bury him in a common grave."

Half an hour later, I found myself driving like a zombie through the streets of Santiago, this unknown young man at my side. Hector, as he was called, had been working in the city morgue for the last week, trying to identify some of the anonymous bodies that were being brought in every day. He was a kind, sensitive young man and he was risking a great deal in coming to find me. As an employee, he had a special identity card and showing it, he ushered me into a small side entrance of the morgue, an unprepossessing building just a few yards from the gates of the General Cemetery.

Even in a state of shock, my body continues to function. Perhaps from outside I look very normal and controlled... my eyes continue to see, my nose to smell, my legs to walk...

We go down a dark passageway and emerge into a large hall. My new friend puts his hand on my elbow to steady me as I look at rows and rows of naked bodies covering the floor, stacked up into heaps in the corners, most with gaping wounds, some with their hands still tied behind their backs... they are young and old... there are hundreds of bodies... most of them look like working people... hundreds of bodies, being sorted out, being dragged by the feet and put into one pile or another, by the people who work in the morgue, strange silent figures with masks across their faces to protect them from the smell of decay. I stand in the center of the room, looking and not wanting to look for Victor, and a great wave of rage assaults me. I know that incoherent noises of protest come from my mouth, but immediately Hector reacts. "Ssh! You mustn't make any sign... otherwise we shall get into trouble... just stay quiet for a moment. I'll go and ask where we should go. I don't think that this is the right place."

We are directed upstairs. The morgue is so full that the bodies overflow to every part of the building, including the administrative offices. A long passage, rows of doors, and on the floor a long line of bodies, these with clothes, some of them look more like students, 10, 20, 30, 40, 50... and there in the middle of the line I find Victor.

It was Victor, although he looked thin and gaunt... What have they done to you to make you waste away like that in one week? His eyes were open and they seemed still to look ahead with intensity and defiance, in spite of a wound on his head and terrible bruises on his cheek. His clothes were torn, trousers round his ankles, sweater tucked up under his armpits, his blue underpants hanging in tatters round his hips as though cut by a knife or bayonet... his chest riddled with holes and a gaping wound in his abdomen. His hands seemed to be hanging from his arms at a strange angle as though his wrists were broken... but it was Victor, my husband, my lover.

Part of me died at that moment too. I felt a whole part of me die as I stood there. Immobile and silent, unable to move, speak.

He should have disappeared. It was only because his face was recognized among hundreds of anonymous bodies that he was not buried in a common grave and I should never have known what had happened to him. I was grateful to the worker who drew attention to him, to young Hector – he was only 19 – who decided to take the risk of coming to find me, who had searched for and found my name and address in the records of *Identificaciones*, asking cooperation of other people in the Identity Bureau. Everyone had helped.

Now it was necessary to claim Victor's body legally. The only way was to take him immediately from the morgue to the cemetery and to bury him... those were the regulations. They made me go home and fetch my marriage certificate. So once more, this time alone, I had to drive across Santiago, now decked with flags for the celebration of Independence Day. I could say nothing to my children yet... the morgue was no place for them, but my friends had been calling, students, wanting to know how we were. One insisted on accompanying me, a good friend... By strange coincidence his name was also Hector.

The paper work, complying with all the regulations, took hours. At 3:00 in the afternoon I was still waiting in the courtyard leading to the basement of the morgue where I was told that Victor's body would be released. Other women were here now, scanning the useless lists that were posted outside, that gave just a number, sex, "no name," found in such and such an area. And as I waited, every few minutes, through the gate from the street came a closed military vehicle with a red cross painted on its side, driving down into the basement, obviously to unload another batch of corpses, and out again to search for more.

At last everything was ready. With the coffin on a trolley we were ready to cross the road to the cemetery. As we came to the gate we met a military vehicle coming in with more corpses. Someone would have to give way. The driver hooted and made furious gestures at us but we stood there silently until he backed out and let Victor's coffin pass.

It must have taken 20 minutes or half an hour to make the long walk to the very end of the cemetery where Victor was to be buried. The trolley squeaked and rattled over the uneven ground. We went on and on, Hector, my new friend, on one side, Hector, my old friend, on the other. Only when Victor's coffin disappeared into the niche that had been allotted to us did I almost collapse. But I was without feeling or sensation. Only the thought of Manuela and Amanda at home, wondering what was happening, wondering where I was, kept me alive.

The next day, the newspaper *La Segunda* published a tiny paragraph which announced Victor's death as though he had passed away peacefully in his bed: "The funeral was private, only relatives were present." Then the order came through to the media not to mention Victor again. But on the television, someone risked their life to insert a few bars of "La plegaria" over the sound track of a U.S. film.

September 15, 1970
President Nixon instructs CIA
Director Richard Helms to
prevent Allende's accession
to office. The CIA is to play
a direct role in organizing
a military coup d'état. This
involvement comes to be
known as Track II.

An Unfinished Song
Joan Jara

It took me months, even years, to piece together something of what happened to Victor during the week that for me he was "missing." Many people could not even speak about their experiences, were afraid to testify, could not bear to remember. Under such horrendous pressure and suffering people lost their sense of time and even of which day of the week events occurred. But gradually, by collecting evidence from Chilean refugees in exile who shared experiences with Victor, were with him at given moments, I have managed to reconstruct, roughly, what he endured while I waited for him at home.

When he reached Plaza Italia on the morning of September 11, Victor found that the center of Santiago had been sealed off by the military, so he turned south down Vicuña McKenna and then west again along Avenida Matta, thus making a wide detour to reach the campus of the Technical University on the far side of the city. He saw the movement of tanks and troops, heard the shooting and explosions, but managed to get through. When he arrived at the Communications Department he learnt that the radio station of the university had been attacked and taken off the air very early that morning by a contingent of armed men from the nearby naval radio station in the Quinta Normal. He must have arrived just about the time that the Moneda Palace was being bombed. From the university buildings it was possible to see the Hawker Hunter jets, to hear the rockets explode as they landed on the Moneda Palace where Allende was holding out and to see the smoke rising from the ruins as the building was destroyed by fire. Soon afterwards, Victor managed to get his turn on an overworked telephone to tell me that he had arrived safely and to ask how we were getting on.

There were about 600 students and teachers gathered in the Technical University that morning. At the opening ceremony, President Allende was to have made an important speech announcing his decision to hold a national plebiscite to resolve by democratic means the conflict threatening the country.

As the first military *bandos* threatened that people on the streets were in danger of being shot and killed and that a curfew was to be enforced from the early hours of the afternoon, Dr. Enrique Kirberg, the rector of the university, negotiated with the military for the people gathered there to stay put all night for their own safety, until the curfew was lifted the next day. This was agreed upon and orders were given for everyone to remain within the university buildings. It was then that Victor must have phoned me for the second time. He didn't tell me that the whole campus was surrounded by tanks and troops.

Through the long hours of the evening, listening to the explosions and heavy machine gun fire all around the neighborhood, they tell me that Victor tried to raise the spirits of the people around him. He sang and got them to sing with him. They had no arms to defend themselves. Then in the staff room of the old building of the Escuela de Artes y Oficios, Victor tried to get some sleep.

All night long the machine gun fire continued. Some people who tried to get out of the university under cover of darkness were shot outright, but it was not until early next morning that the assault began in earnest, with the tanks firing their heavy guns against the buildings, damaging the structure of some, shattering windows and destroying laboratories, equipment, books. There was no answering fire, because there were no guns inside.

After the tanks had crashed into the university precincts, the troops proceeded to herd all the people, including the rector, out into a large courtyard normally used for sport. Using rifle butts and boots to kick and beat people, they forced everyone to lie on the ground, hands on the backs of their heads. Victor was there with the others; perhaps it was on the way out of the building that he had got rid of his identity card in the hope that he might not be recognized.

After lying there for more than an hour, they were made to get into single file and trot, still with their hands on their heads, to the Estadio Chile, about six blocks away, subjected to insults, kicks and blows on the way. It was when they were lining up outside the stadium that Victor was first recognized by one of the non-commissioned officers. "You're that fucking singer, aren't you?" and he hit Victor on the head, felling him, then kicking him in the stomach and ribs. Victor was separated from the others as they entered the building and put into a special gallery, reserved for "important" or "dangerous" prisoners. His friends saw him from afar, remembered the wide smile that he flashed at them from across the horror that they were witnessing, in spite of a bloody face and a wound in his head. Later they saw him curl up across the seats, his hands tucked beneath his armpits against the penetrating cold.

Some time next morning, Victor evidently decided to try to leave his isolated position and join the other prisoners. Another witness, who was waiting in the passageway outside, saw the following scene. As Victor pushed the swing doors to come out into the passageway, he almost bumped into an army officer who seemed to be the second-in-command of the stadium. He had been very busy shouting over the microphone, giving orders, screaming threats. He was tall, blond and rather handsome and was obviously enjoying the role he was playing as he strutted about. Some of the prisoners had already nicknamed him "the Prince."

As Victor came face to face with him, he gave a sign of recognition and smiled sarcastically. Mimicking playing a guitar, he giggled and then quickly drew his finger across his throat. Victor remained calm and made some gesture in reply, but then the officer shouted, "What is this bastard doing here?" He called the guards who were following him and said, "Don't let him move from here. This one is reserved for me!"

Later, Victor was transferred to the basement where there are glimpses of him in a passageway, there where he had so often prepared to sing, now lying, covered in blood, on a floor running with urine and excrement overflowing from the toilet.

In the evening he was brought back into the main part of the stadium to join the other prisoners. He could scarcely walk, his head and his face were bloody and bruised, one of his ribs seemed to be broken and he was in pain where he had been kicked in the stomach. His friends wiped his face and tried to make him more comfortable. One of them had a small jar of jam and some biscuits. They shared the food between three or four of them, dipping their fingers into the jam one after the other and licking every vestige of it.

The next day, Friday, September 14, the prisoners were divided into groups of about 200, ready to be transferred to the National Stadium. It was then that Victor, slightly recovered, asked his friends if anyone had a pencil and paper and he began to write his last poem. Some of the worst horrors of the military coup took place in the Estadio Chile in those first days before it was visited by the Red Cross, Amnesty International or representatives of foreign embassies. (In spite of legal proceedings and inquiries by lawyers, I have never been able to discover the names of the officers who were in command of the Estadio Chile.)

Thousands of prisoners were kept for days, with virtually no food or water; glaring spotlights were focused on them constantly so that they lost all sense of time and even of day and night; machine guns were set up all around the stadium and were fired intermittently either at the ceiling or over the heads the prisoners; orders and threats were blared over loudspeakers. The commanding officer was a corpulent man and only his silhouette could be seen as he warned that the machine guns we nicknamed "Hitler's saws" because they could cut a man in half... and would do so as necessary. Prisoners were called out one by one, made to move from one part of the stadium to another. It was impossible to rest. People were

mercilessly beaten with whips and rifle butts. One man who could
no longer bear it threw himself over the balcony and plunged to
his death among the prisoners below. Others had attacks of madness
and were gunned down in full view of everybody.

As Victor scribbled, he was trying to record, for the world to
know, something of the horror that had been let loose in Chile.
He could only testify to his "small corner of the city," where 5,000
people were imprisoned, could only imagine what must be happening in the rest of his country. He must have realized the monstrous
scale of the military operation, the precision with which it had
been prepared.

In those last hours of his life, deep roots of his peasant child-
hood made him see the military as "midwives," whose coming was
the signal for screams and what had seemed to him, as a child,
unbearable suffering. Now these visions became confused with
the torture and the sadistic smile of "the Prince." But even then,
Victor still had hope for the future, confidence that people were
stronger, in the end, than bombs and machine guns... and as he
came to the last verses, for which he already had music inside him
– "How hard it is to sing, when I must sing of horror..." – he was
interrupted. A group of guards came to fetch him, to separate
him from those who were about to be transferred to the National
Stadium. He quickly passed the scrap of paper to a *compañero* who
was sitting beside him, who in turn hid it in his sock as he was
taken away. His friends had tried, each one of them, to learn the
poem by heart as it was written, so as to carry it out of the stadium
with them. They never saw Victor again.

In spite of the fact that large numbers were transferred to other
prison camps, the Estadio Chile remained full because more and
more prisoners were constantly arriving, both men and women.
I have two more glimpses of Victor in the stadium, two more tes-
timonies... a message for me brought out by someone who was
near him for some hours, down in the dressing rooms, converted
now into torture chambers, a message of love for his daughters
and for me... then once more being publicly abused and beaten,
the officer nicknamed "the Prince" shouting at him, on the verge
of hysteria, losing control of himself: "Sing now, if you can, you

bastard!" and Victor's voice raised in the stadium after those four days of suffering, to sing a verse of the Popular Unity hymn, "Venceremos." Then he was beaten down and dragged away for the last phase of his agony.

The boxing stadium lies within a few yards of the main railway line to the south, which, on its way out of Santiago, passes through the working-class district of San Miguel, along the boundary wall of the Metropolitan Cemetery. It was here early in the morning of Sunday, September 16, that the people of the *población* found six dead bodies, lying in an orderly row. All had terrible wounds and had been machine gunned to death.

They looked from face to face, trying to recognize the corpses and suddenly one of the women cried out, "This is Victor Jara!" – it was a face which was both known and dear to them. One of the women even knew Victor personally because when he had visited the *población* to sing, she had invited him into her home to eat a plate of beans. Almost immediately, while they were wondering what to do, a covered van approached. The people of the *población* quickly hid behind a wall, in fear, but watched while a group of men in plain clothes began dragging the corpses by the feet and throwing them into the van. From here Victor's body must have been transferred to the city morgue, an anonymous corpse, ready to disappear into a mass grave. But once again, he was recognized – by one of the people who worked there.

When later the text of his last poem was brought to me, I knew that Victor wanted to leave his testimony, his only means now of resisting fascism, of fighting for the rights of human beings and for peace.

October 24, 1970
the Chilean Congress votes 153 to 35
to endorse Allende as president.

Estadio Chile

Victor Jara

There are five thousand of us here
in this small part of the city.
We are five thousand.
I wonder how many we are in all
in the cities and in the whole country?
Here alone
are ten thousand hands which plant seeds
and make the factories run.
How much humanity
exposed to hunger, cold, panic, pain,
moral pressures, terror and insanity?
Six of us were lost
as if into starry space.
One dead, another beaten as I could never have believed
a human being could be beaten.
The other four wanted to end their terror –
one jumping into nothingness,
another beating his head against a wall,
but all with the fixed stare of death.
What horror the face of fascism creates!
They carry out their plans with knife-like precision.
Nothing matters to them.
For them, blood equals medals,

slaughter is an act of heroism.
Oh God, is this the world that you created,
for this, your seven days of wonder and work?

Within these four walls only a number exists
which does not progress,
which slowly will wish more and more for death.
But suddenly my conscience awakes
and I see that this tide has no heartbeat,
only the pulse of machines
and the military showing their midwives' faces
full of sweetness.
Let Mexico, Cuba and the world
cry out against this atrocity!
We are ten thousand hands
which can produce nothing.
How many of us in the whole country?

The blood of our president, our *compañero*,
will strike with more strength than bombs and machine guns!
So will our fist strike again!
How hard it is to sing
when I must sing of horror.
Horror which I am living,
horror which I am dying.
To see myself among so much
and so many moments of infinity
in which silence and screams
are the end of my song.
What I see, I have never seen
What I have felt and what I feel
will give birth to the moment...

Estadio Chile
September 1973
Translated from the Spanish by Joan Jara

"We Never Saw Him Hesitate,"
September 28, 1973
Beatriz Allende

Beatriz Allende was the daughter of President Salvador Allende. She fled Chile after the coup and lived in Cuba where after years of torment she took her own life in 1977. In this speech, given in 1973 just days after the coup, she addresses a Cuban audience.

I am not here to deliver a speech. I am simply here to tell this people who have always shown us so much solidarity about the last hours we experienced at La Moneda Palace on the morning of September 11.

I am here to tell you about the attitudes and the lines of action and thought of comrade President Salvador Allende when confronted with the attack of the treacherous and fascist military.

The Cuban people, of course, know the truth, but in many other countries the campaign of lies staged by the fascist junta, backed by agencies of U.S. imperialism, tries to draw a curtain over the events which took place at La Moneda, President Allende's battle trench.

I am here to confirm for you that the president of Chile fought with weapons in hand to the end; that he defended to the last breath the mandate his people had given him – a mandate for the Chilean Revolution, a mandate for socialism.

President Salvador Allende fell under enemy fire as a soldier of the revolution, without yielding at any time, with complete confidence, with the optimism of someone who knows the people of Chile will overcome any setback and will fight without truce until full and final victory. He died with unwavering confidence in the people's strength, fully aware of the historic meaning of his position – defending with his life the cause of the workers and the poor of his country.

Both Cuba and Fidel were in his words and in his heart in those difficult moments. We witnessed, until his death, the loyalty and deep affection binding him to the Cuban people, the Cuban Revolution and Fidel Castro.

We lived on constant guard for almost the entire month before the September 11 coup. There wasn't a day without rumors about a military uprising or a coup d'état. That morning of Tuesday, September 11, we received disturbing news and learned that President Allende had gone to the palace in the early hours. We went there without yet realizing the importance of what was taking place.

It was only while on the way to La Moneda, when several times we had to avoid the *Carabineros'* barriers that were blocking the way in an openly hostile manner, that we understood the seriousness of the situation. We were able to reach La Moneda at approximately 8:50 a.m. There was the usual *Carabinero* guard inside, whose duty it was to protect the palace. Nevertheless, before entering the building, we had seen *Carabineros* in the vicinity who were surrendering or joining the coup.

At La Moneda we immediately confirmed that it was a full coup d'état, with the participation of the three branches of the armed forces and the *Carabineros.*

Inside the building, preparations for combat were under way. The president was flanked by a larger than usual group of his personal guard, who had taken up combat positions. The few heavy weapons had been distributed. In addition, there was a group of men from the Investigations Service who had always worked in coordination with the personal guard.

Also present was a group of ministers, undersecretaries, former ministers, technicians and radio and news journalists, as well as doctors, nurses, and the La Moneda administrative staff – those who didn't want to leave and had decided instead to fight at Allende's side. Finally, the closest members of his own staff were there, 11 of them women.

I saw him for the first time that day when I handed over to him one of the many telephone calls coming in. He was serene, calmly listening to the different reports brought in and giving orders and answers that left no room for disagreement. He had already personally inspected – he would inspect them on several other occasions – the combat positions, correcting the firing angle of several comrades.

Soon the infantry fire, the tank and artillery attack on the Presidential Palace by the coup forces would begin. Our comrades fired back.

We learned that early that day the military *golpistas* had already repeatedly urged the president to give up, but he always refused, bluntly and irrevocably, to accept their ultimatums. We never saw him hesitate. On the contrary, he continuously reaffirmed his decision to fight to the end without surrendering to the treasonous military, whom he already called by their true names: fascists.

I also learned that he had received visits that morning and would continue to receive calls from the parties of Popular Unity and the Movement of the Revolutionary Left, expressing their decision to fight.

One of the traitorous generals, by the name of Baeza, called him on several occasions. I also learned that the coup forces had offered him a plane, which would take him, his family and members of his staff anywhere he wanted. The president replied that traitorous generals such as themselves were incapable of knowing what an honorable man was, and dismissed them angrily, using very strong language.

The president was taking measures to engage in a long battle. He moved continuously from one place to another. He asked for a check of the most sheltered places to protect the fighters from future air raids. He kept informed as to the food and water supply.

He ordered the medical group to have the surgery ward

ready to care for the wounded. He told one comrade to gather the women together and take them to a safe place. He ordered the destruction of documents that might jeopardize other revolutionaries, even personal documents. He sent three comrades, two of them women, out on a mission to help the future resistance.

We then learned that the *Carabineros* in charge of protecting the palace had joined the fascist junta.

I was able to talk to the president alone for a moment. He repeated that he would fight to the end; that it was perfectly obvious to him what was going to happen, but that he was going to take measures so that the battle could be carried out in the best possible manner. It was going to be difficult, under adverse conditions. He added, however, that he was aware this was the only position he could take as a revolutionary and as the constitutional president defending the authority which the people had given him. By not surrendering or giving in, he would expose all the fascist and traitorous military.

He was worried about the other women who were in the palace and about his other daughter, Isabel. He wanted all of them to leave the palace and for us to take care of our mother, because there was fighting at Tomás Moro, and she was there.

Then he told me that, in a way, the fact that this moment had arrived had unburdened his shoulders. In this way, he said, things were cleared up and he was freed of the situation which had disturbed him lately: that while being the president of a people's government, the armed forces, under cover of the so-called Arms Control Act, were at the same time repressing and abusing the workers, and breaking into factories. He had told me this on other occasions.

He was in extraordinary spirits and eager to engage in battle. His remarks reflected a coolheaded view of events, and the course that the revolutionary struggle would necessarily take. He said that the important thing was future political leadership, guaranteeing a united leadership for all revolutionary forces, because the workers would need a united political leadership. That is why he didn't want useless sacrifices. Efforts had to be made to obtain a united political leadership to head the resistance that would begin that very day, and clear-sighted political leadership would be needed for this.

He told the same thing to the ministers and other members of his staff whom he gathered in the Toesca Room. He reiterated his determination to defend presidential authority even at the cost of his life, and thanked them for their cooperation during the past three years. The men who were armed were ordered to go back to their places of battle, and the unarmed ones were to go with the president to help convince the women to leave La Moneda, and then do so themselves, because he didn't want useless sacrifices when the important thing would be the organization and leadership of the working class...

The women and other comrades spent the last moments near the surgery ward and in a small underground room where paper was stored. The president went there with his olive green military helmet. He was carrying an AK automatic rifle that had been a gift from Fidel, with the inscription, "To my comrade-in-arms."

We would soon be bombed. The planes were flying over at very low altitudes. Very firmly, he ordered us to leave the palace immediately, with no more delays. He spoke to each of us individually, explaining why we would be more useful outside, and our revolutionary commitment to be fulfilled.

He again said that the important thing was organization, unity and political leadership for his people.

He reproached me for being there when I was pregnant, that my duty was to go to the comrades of the Cuban Embassy. He told me he had felt the provocations and attacks against the Cuban Embassy during the last few months as if they were attacks on him personally. He thought they might be provoked that day and that there might be fighting, and that is why I should be with them.

He took us to the exit on Morandé Street. There, he called for a halt in the firing and organized a military jeep so the women could get out without any problems. A few minutes before that, he had considered the possibility that we would be held as hostages again to demand his surrender. But he said if this happened then he would not hesitate; that to the contrary, it would be one more piece of evidence to show the people of Chile and the world how far fascism's treachery and shame could go and that for him it would be one more reason for fighting.

That is how we left him just before the bombing, fighting with a small group of revolutionaries and one of the women who had hidden in order to stay behind to fight with them. Comrades, this is the image I retain of the president. Dear Cuban brothers and sisters, this is the image I would like to leave in your hearts and minds.

This image rises over this plaza with revolutionary pride, where only a few months ago he raised his deeply-moved voice to express to you the solidarity and gratitude of our country, our workers, our children, women and old people.

At this rally of solidarity with Chile, I want to repeat what he asked me to tell you. In La Moneda in the midst of battle, he said, "Tell Fidel I will do my duty. Tell him we must have the best possible united political leadership for the people of Chile." He said this day marked the beginning of a long resistance, and that Cuba and all revolutionaries would have to aid us in it.

"The battle until death against fascism has started, and it will end the day we have the free, sovereign and socialist Chile for which you fought and gave your life."

Today, from this, the first free territory in the Americas, we can tell comrade Allende: your people will not surrender, your people will not fold the flag of revolution; the battle until death against fascism has started, and it will end the day we have the free, sovereign and socialist Chile for which you fought and gave your life.

1971

Neither the Inter-American
Development Bank nor the
World Bank grants new credits
to Chile after Allende assumes
the presidency, even denying
emergency relief to victims
of the earthquake.

Death of a Poet

Matilde Urrutia Neruda and Joan Jara

Matilde Urrutia Neruda

One could say that Pablo was a happy man. This could be per-
cieved in everything he wrote, even when he was forced to keep
to his bed.

He had somewhat recovered from his illness, but the day of
the coup d'état was a very trying one for him. When we learned
of Salvador Allende's death, the doctor called me immediately
and said: "Keep all the news from Pablo, for it could put him
beyond recovery."

Pablo had a TV set in front of his bed. He would send his
driver to fetch all the newspapers. He also had a radio that got all
the news. We heard of Allende's death through a Mendoza
(Argentinean) station, and this announcement killed him. Yes, it
killed him.

On the day following Allende's death, Pablo awoke in a fever,
with no access to medical care, because the head doctor had
been arrested and his assistant did not dare to go as far as Isla
Negra. Thus we were isolated without medical help. The days
were passing and Pablo's condition was growing worse. At the
end of the fifth day, I called the physician and told him, "We must

take him to a clinic. He is seriously ill."

All day he was riveted to the radio – listening to stations in Venezuela, Argentina and the Soviet Union. Finally, he grasped the situation.

His mind was perfectly lucid – absolutely clear till he fell asleep.

At the end of five days I called a private ambulance to take him to a Santiago clinic. The vehicle was thoroughly searched during the trip, which disturbed him greatly. There were other brutalities, and that also affected him visibly. I was at his side. They made me get out, and searched me and the ambulance. It was terrible for him. I kept telling them: "It's Pablo Neruda. He is very ill. Let us through." It was frightful, and he reached the clinic in a critical condition.

Pablo died at 10:30 p.m. and no one was able to go to the clinic because of the curfew. I then had him transported to his Santiago home, which had been destroyed – books, everything. There we kept watch, and many people came, in spite of the times we were passing through in Santiago.

When we arrived at the cemetery, people came from everywhere, workers, all workers with hard, serious faces. Half of them kept shouting, "Pablo Neruda," and the other half replied: "Present." This crowd entered the cemetery singing the "Internationale" in spite of the repression.

Joan Jara

Hundreds of people had gathered to honor Neruda, in spite of the soldiers lining the streets, machine guns threatening, at the ready, and the secret police scanning the crowd for wanted faces. Quena and I started off fairly near the front of the procession, but gradually lagged further and further behind because I seemed incapable of walking faster; it cost me to put one foot in front of the other. As we walked through the back streets towards the cemetery, I heard Neruda's poetry being recited by one person after another in the crowd, verse after verse, defying the menace of the uniforms surrounding us; I saw the workers: on a building site, standing to attention with their yellow helmets in their hands, high above us on a scaffolding; others lined the pavement with the soldiers hemming us in.

"*Sube a nacer conmigo, hermano,*" ("Arise to be born with me, my brother") and "Come and see the blood in the streets..." Neruda's verses took on an even greater significance as voice after voice took them up, confronting the visible face of fascism. As I walked, I knew I was not alone, I knew that this was also Victor's funeral and that of all those *compañeros* who had been massacred by the military, many of them flung anonymously into common graves. The presence of dozens of foreign journalists, film crews, television cameras, protected us from aggression and interference, but as the procession reached the last stage of the march at the rotunda in front of the main gates of the cemetery, a military convoy with armored trucks rounded it in the opposite direction, looming over us. The crowd respond with cries of "*Compañero Pablo Neruda: Presente, ahora y siempre!*" "*Compañera Salvador Allende: Presente, ahora y siempra!*" and then breaking into "The Internationale," raggedly, nervous at first, but then with more strength as everyone started to sing. It was Popular Unity's last public demonstration in Chile, the first public demonstration of resistance to a fascist regime.

et those who want to turn back the
lock of history and ignore the will
of the majority of the people realize
hat even though I am not inclined
o being a martyr, I will not retreat."
Salvador Allende

Portrait of the Man

Pablo Neruda

It is necessary to judge those hands stained
by the dead he killed with his terror;

the dead from under the earth
are rising up like seeds of sorrow.

Because this is a time never before dreamed of.

And Nixon, the trapped rat,
his eyes wide with fear,
is watching the rebirth of flags shot down.

He was defeated every day in Vietnam.
In Cuba his rage was driven away
and now in the buried twilight
this rodent is gnawing at Chile
not knowing that Chileans of little importance
are going to give him a lesson in honor.

The Andes
for Pablo Neruda

David Ray

Neruda
they dig to the Andes' spine
with augers as crooked as Nixon's shoes –
like a silkworm it spins
so smooth it is
and out of the mountain they make
their kimono –
the brocade on Madame Nixon's dragon
flakes on the floor, nitrates,
cobalt, diamond dust, oil
that rolls in tiny droplets like an insect's tears.
And they whittle at your spine
knowing there's something there
something valuable, maybe gold
maybe radioactive
something they can use
words locked in the bone.

Neruda, The Wine

Muriel Rukeyser

We are the seas through whom the great fish passed
And passes. He died in a moment of general dying.
Something was reborn. What was it, Pablo?
Something is being reborn: poems, death, ourselves
The link dead in our peoples, the dead link in our dead regimes,
The last of our encounters transformed from the first
Long ago in Xavier's house, where you lay sick,
Speaking of poems, the sheet pushed away
Growth of beard pressing up, fierce grass, as you spoke.
And that last moment in the hall of students,
Speaking at last of Spain, the core of all our lives,
The long defeat that brings us what we know.
Meaning, poems, lifelong in loss and preference, passing forever.
I spilled the wine at the table
And you, Pablo, dipped your fingers in it and marked my forehead.
Words, blood, rivers, cities, days. I go, a woman marked by you –
The poems of the wine.

On the Coup in Chile
Fidel Castro

Fidel Castro delivered this speech at the same Havana rally, on September 28, 1973,
which was addressed by Beatriz Allende [see page 35], days after the coup.

Less than 10 months ago in this same plaza, on December 13,
1972, our people had their last meeting with President Allende.
Hundreds of thousands of Cubans met with him here to hear his
magnificent words and to express our confidence, fellowship,
and support for Allende and the revolutionary process in Chile.
We expressed our determination to support him as much as we
could, and demonstrated as such with a gesture we know deeply
touched President Allende's heart: our decision to give up a little
of our own food so we could send it to the Chilean people.

We remember how happy the president was during those
short days of his visit here; he felt himself among friends, among
true brothers and sisters, among his family... It was in this same
plaza we became convinced he would behave as a revolutionary in
times of crisis, and here that he told us the Chilean people would
answer counterrevolutionary violence with revolutionary violence.

President Allende and the Chilean revolutionary process
awakened great interest and solidarity throughout the world. In
Chile, for the first time in history, a new experience developed:
the attempt to bring about the revolution by peaceful, legal
means. He had the understanding and support of all the world in

his effort – not only of the international communist movement, but of very different political tendencies as well.

Our party and people – in spite of the fact that we had made our revolution by other means – and all the other revolutionary peoples in the world supported him. We didn't hesitate with our support for one minute, because we understood there was a possibility in Chile of winning an electoral victory, in spite of imperialism's resources and those of the ruling classes; in spite of all the adverse circumstances. We didn't hesitate in 1970 to publicly state our agreement and support of the efforts the Chilean left was making to win the elections that year.

And, sure enough, there was an electoral victory. The left, Popular Unity, with its social and political programs, won at the polls. Of course, that didn't mean the triumph of a revolution; it meant access to very important positions of power by peaceful, legal means.

It wasn't, however, an easy task that Allende was faced with. There were conspiracies from the beginning. An attempt was made to keep him from being inaugurated after the elections, when imperialism and its agencies – the CIA and multinational companies – conspired to keep Salvador Allende from becoming president of the republic. They murdered the commander of the Chilean Army in attempting to prevent it. Former President Frei, an arrogant and profoundly reactionary man, wasn't resigned to having Salvador Allende occupy the presidency, as had been decided by the people's vote.

Yet in spite of the conspiracies, in spite of imperialism's efforts, Salvador Allende, in the name of Popular Unity, took office.

What problems confronted him? A bourgeois state apparatus was firmly intact. The armed forces called themselves apolitical, institutional – that is, apparently neutral in the revolutionary process. There was a bourgeois parliament, where a majority of members jumped to the tune of the ruling classes. The judicial system was completely subservient to the reactionaries. The country's economy was also completely bankrupt and the Chilean state was $4 billion in debt. It was in those circumstances that Allende had to carry out his governmental duties.

That huge debt was the product of imperialist policies, the product of U.S. engineering, which was trying to create a showcase of a Christian Democratic government so as to confront and halt the advance of the social movement.

When Frei was president, the United States granted Chile huge loans. But they weren't loans to aid development of the country; they were loans for lavish consumption – for cars, television sets, refrigerators and all kinds of other consumer goods which gave an image of progress and well-being to the Christian Democratic government.

President Allende found himself with a country heavily burdened by debt; a country in which imperialism had introduced its customs and its consumer habits; a country in which the mass media – the press, television and radio – was in the hands of the oligarchy. It was a time when the price of copper plummeted from 75 cents to 48 cents a pound.

Moreover, the people had crying needs that simply had to be met, such as large-scale unemployment. The demands most felt by the population had to be attended to, and the Popular Unity government found enormous economic obstacles in its path. When agrarian reform began to be put into effect, large landowners and the agrarian bourgeoisie immediately started sabotaging agricultural production. The bourgeoisie – owners of the distribution centers, warehouses and stores – cornered the market, sabotaging the Popular Unity government.

As soon as the nationalization of the copper enterprises was approved – that had extracted millions of dollars from the labor and sweat of the Chilean people – imperialism froze all loans granted by all international organizations to the Chilean government and went about stifling the economy of Chile.

The bourgeois political parties – essentially the National Party and the Christian Democratic Party – took it upon themselves, in complicity with imperialism and the reactionary classes and with the reactionary press, to place obstacles in the way of everything President Allende tried to do, making it practically impossible for him to govern; they virtually tied the hands of the government to keep it from doing anything.

Those three years of the Popular Unity government were really three years of struggles, difficulties and agony as it attempted to carry out its program. Three years of one plot after another, conspiracy after conspiracy. Owners, merchants and even professionals – the kinds of professionals we knew here, most of them at the service of the ruling classes, sabotaged the government's tasks: they called work stoppages and strikes and completely paralyzed the country on more than one occasion. This wasn't all. They continually called on the armed forces to overthrow the Popular Unity government.

President Allende kept working in the midst of these tremendous difficulties. He tried to do – and did do – many things for the Chilean people. Throughout those three years, the Chilean people – especially the workers and farmers – understood that there was in the presidency of the republic a representative not of the oligarchs, large landowners and bourgeoisie but of the poor and the workers – a true representative of the people, for whom he was fighting, in spite of the enormous difficulties he faced.

President Allende realized the difficulties and foresaw the dangers; he was witnessing the birth of fascism. All that he had to oppose those forces, which had been created and spurred on by imperialism, was his fighting spirit and determination to defend the process at the cost of his very life.

We recall what he said, in a clear and decisive manner, on the afternoon of December 4, 1971, in a stadium in the city of Santiago, at a farewell rally for the Cuban delegation:

> ...I tell you calmly, with absolute tranquillity, I am not an apostle or a messiah. I do not have the spirit of a martyr. I am a social fighter fulfilling a task given him by the people. Let those who want to turn back the clock of history and ignore the will of the majority of the people realize that even though I am not inclined to being a martyr, I will not retreat. They must realize that I will only leave La Moneda when I fulfil the people's mandate.
>
> They must realize this, they must listen well and let it sink into their heads: I will defend this Chilean Revolution and I will defend the people's government, because it is the mandate that the people have given me. I have no other alternative. Only by

> pumping me with bullets will they be able to keep me from fulfilling
> the program of the people.

That wasn't just rhetoric. It showed the will and determination of
a man of honor.

Salvador Allende kept his word, dramatically and impressively!

The fascists have tried to keep the events of September 11
from becoming public knowledge. With the reports of some of
the survivors who were with the president that morning, we have
established what happened on September 11 around President
Allende. Allende's daughter, who gave us a clear account of everything she saw and heard that day, next to her father, also provided
some information. Her words centered on President Allende's
humane side, his concern over the comrades who were unarmed
or who might be killed there uselessly – since he was aware of the
need for cadres and leaders to aid in the future struggle. How
right he was!

If Comrade Beatriz Allende had been killed that day in La
Moneda Palace, the one million people here, and the world's
public as a whole, would never have known about Allende's gestures, concerns and worries, and especially about his great pre-
occupation with the unity of revolutionary forces, his call for
unity and his feelings and unshakable determination to fight to
the death in defense of his just cause. Now we know what
President Allende's attitude was and what spirits he was in that day.

At 6:20 a.m. that day, the president received a telephone call at
his Tomás Moro residence informing him of the military coup taking place. Immediately, he alerted his personal guard and made the
firm decision to go to La Moneda Palace to defend the Popular
Unity government in his post as president of the republic. With him
were 23 bodyguards, armed with 23 automatic rifles, two .30 caliber
machine guns, and three bazookas. They went to the Presidential
Palace in four cars and one pickup truck, arriving there at 7:30 a.m.

Carrying his automatic rifle, the president, accompanied by
his bodyguards, entered the main gate of La Moneda. At this time,
there was the usual *Carabinero* protection in the palace.

Once inside, he called a meeting, informing those with him

that the situation was very serious and telling them of his decision
to fight until death defending the legitimate and popular constitutional government of Chile against the fascist coup. He examined
the available weapons and gave the first instructions for the
defense of the palace.

Seven men from the Investigations Service arrived to join the
defenders. The *Carabineros*, meanwhile, were in their places, and
some of them took measures to defend the building. A small
group of personal bodyguards guarded the entrance to the presidential office, with instructions not to let any armed military
officer enter, to avoid any acts of treason.

Within the space of one hour, he spoke to the Chilean people
three times over the radio, expressing his will to resist.

Just after 8:15 a.m., the fascist junta, using the palace's intercom
system, urged the president to surrender and to give up his office,
offering him an airplane in which to leave the country with his
family and colleagues. Allende told them, "As traitorous generals,
you are incapable of knowing what honorable men are like," and
indignantly rejected the ultimatum.

The president had a brief meeting in his office with several
high officials of the *Carabineros* who had gone to the palace. They
cowardly refused to defend the government. The president dismissed them with contempt, ordering them to leave the palace
immediately. While this meeting with the *Carabinero* officers was
taking place, the three military aides-de-camp arrived. The president
told them it was not the moment for trusting men in military uniforms, and asked them to leave La Moneda.

Minutes after the aides-de-camp and the *Carabinero* officials
left, the commanding lieutenant of the *Carabinero* garrison at the
Presidential Palace, taking orders from his headquarters, instructed
one *Carabinero* to go through the building and order the garrison
men to withdraw. These men immediately began to leave La
Moneda, taking some of the weapons with them. The *Carabineros'*
armored trucks, which up until that moment were stationed in
front of the palace in defense positions, followed suit.

A group of 10 *Carabineros*, accompanied by the bearer of the
withdrawal order and, no doubt, following instructions, turned

their rifles on the president as they were leaving by the main stairway and nearing the exit. The president's personal bodyguards shot back, engaging in the first shooting with those military carrying out the coup.

While these events were taking place, numerous ministers, undersecretaries, advisers, the president's daughters Beatriz and Isabel, and other members of Popular Unity, had been arriving at the palace to be at the president's side at this critical time.

At approximately 9:15 a.m., the first shots were fired at the palace from outside. Fascist infantry troops, numbering over 200 men, were moving along Teatinos and Morandé streets, on either side of the Plaza de la Constitución, toward the Presidential Palace, firing at the president's office. The forces defending the palace did not exceed 40 men.

The fascists then brought in tanks, supported by the infantry. A tank moved along Moneda Street, another along Teatinos, another along Alameda at the corner of Morandé and another along the Plaza de la Constitución toward the main door. At that moment, from the president's own office, bazooka fire opened upon the tank at the main door, destroying it completely. Two other tanks aimed their fire at the president's office, and an armored truck shot at the private secretary's office and that of the bodyguards with their machine guns. Several artillery detachments located on the side of the Plaza de la Constitución also fired at the palace. The president went to the different combat positions, encouraging and leading the defenders. The fierce struggle continued for more than one hour, and the fascists were unable to move forward an inch.

At 10:45 a.m., the president met in the Toesca Room with the ministers, undersecretaries, and advisers who had come to the palace to be at his side. He told them that the future struggle would need leaders and cadres, that all those who were unarmed should abandon the La Moneda Palace as soon as possible, and all those who were armed should continue at their combat posts. Of course, none of the unarmed agreed, and neither the president's daughters nor the other women at La Moneda wanted to leave the palace.

The battle was fierce. Over the palace's intercom system the fascists furiously issued new ultimatums, announcing that if the defenders did not give up, they would immediately send in the air force.

At 11:45 a.m., the president met with his daughters and the other nine women at the palace, firmly ordering them to leave La Moneda, since he thought it senseless for them to die there without being able to defend themselves. He immediately asked for a three-minute ceasefire from the besiegers, in order to evacuate the women. The fascists did not agree to the truce, but their troops began to withdraw from the vicinity of the palace at this time, in order to launch the air attack, and this brought about an impasse in the fight which allowed the women to leave.

At about 12:00 noon, the air attack began on the palace. The first rockets went through the roof and exploded in the Winter Courtyard, located in the center of the building. More air raids and rockets followed one after the other, filling the whole building with smoke and toxic fumes. The president gave orders to get all the gas masks, noted how much ammunition was left, and urged all fighters to staunchly resist the air raid.

The president's bodyguards were running out of ammunition for their automatic rifles after almost three hours of fighting, so the president ordered that the door to the palace *Carabinero* garrison's armory be broken down, since some arms were stored there. Growing impatient over the delay in information about the weapons, he crossed the Winter Courtyard and went to the armory himself, where he ordered that hand grenades be used in the operation. A hole was opened in the door of the armory, and four .30-caliber machine guns, numerous Sik rifles, and a lot of ammunition, gas masks and helmets were brought out. The president ordered that all this be immediately taken to the firing line, and he toured the *Carabinero* dormitories, picking up what Sik rifles and other weapons he found there.

Carrying numerous weapons on his shoulders to reinforce the combat positions, the president said, "That is how we write the first page of this history. My people and the people of the Americas will write the rest."

While the president was carrying arms and ammunition from the armory, the air attack was renewed. An explosion shattered the windows near where the president was stationed, and he was wounded in the back by fragments of glass. This was the first wound he suffered. While being treated for his wound, he ordered the transfer of arms to continue. He was always concerned about the fate of his comrades.

A few minutes later, the fascists resumed their attack, joining the planes with artillery, tanks and infantry. According to witnesses, the noise, shelling, explosions, smoke and noxious gases turned the palace into an inferno. Although the president had ordered that all the water pipes be opened to prevent fires on the ground floor, a fire started on the left side of the palace and spread to the aides' room and the Red Room. In spite of this, the president wasn't discouraged, not even in the most critical period, and ordered that the massive attack be countered with all possible means.

Then Allende, with the palace in flames and under fire, crawled to his office on Plaza de la Constitución, took a bazooka, aimed at a tank on Morandé Street which was firing at the palace and put it out of action with a direct hit. A few minutes later, another fighter put a third tank out of action.

The fascists brought in new armored cars, troops, and tanks along Morandé Street, increasing their fire against the door of the La Moneda Palace. Fire continued to rage in the palace. The president and several other fighters went to the ground floor to throw back the fascists' attempt to enter the palace from Morandé Street, and this was accomplished.

Then the fascists halted their fire in that sector and shouted for two representatives of the government to come out for a parley. The president sent Flores, general secretary of the government, and Daniel Vergara, deputy secretary of the interior, who went out through the door on Morandé Street and approached a military jeep that was stationed in front. This was at about 1:00 p.m. Flores and Vergara talked with a high-ranking officer in the jeep. On their return to the palace, when they were near the door, they were fired on from the jeep. Flores was hit in the right leg, and Daniel Vergara was hit in the back several times and was dragged into the palace while other defenders gave covering fire.

The fascists had requested the parley again to demand surrender. They offered the president and the defenders facilities to
leave the palace and go anywhere they wanted. The president
immediately reiterated his determination to fight to the last. On the
ground floor they resisted the attack that came from Morandé Street.
The main entrance to the palace was already practically destroyed.

At about 1:30 p.m. the president went back up to the second
floor. By then, many of the defenders had been killed by the
shelling and explosions or been burned to death. Journalist
Augusto Olivares amazed everyone with his extraordinary heroism. Seriously wounded, he was taken away and operated on in
the palace's medical room, but, when everyone thought he was
still lying there, he grabbed a weapon and came back to fight
along with the president on the second floor. The names of the
fighters who distinguished themselves there and their acts of
heroism are endless.

After 1:30 p.m. the fascists took over the ground floor of the
palace; the defense was organized on the second floor, and the
battle continued. The fascists tried to break through via the main
staircase. At about 2:00 p.m. they managed to occupy a corner of
the second floor. The president and several of his comrades had
barricaded themselves in a corner of the Red Room. Advancing to
where the fascists had broken through, the president was shot in
the stomach. The pain doubled him up, but he didn't stop fighting.
Supporting himself in a chair, he kept shooting at the fascists, who
were only a few yards away, until a second bullet got him in the
chest, the impact threw him to the floor and, already dying, he was
riddled with bullets.

Seeing the president fall, the members of his personal body-
guard launched a powerful counterattack and fought the fascists
back to the main staircase. Then, in the midst of combat, there was
an amazing gesture of dignity: they took the body of the president
to his office, sat it in the presidential chair, placed the president's
sash on it, and wrapped Allende's body in a Chilean flag.

Even after their president was dead, those immortal defenders
of the palace resisted the savage fascist attacks for two more

hours. It was only at 4:00 in the afternoon, when the Presidential Palace had been burning for several hours, that the last resistance was put down.

Many will be amazed by what has just been narrated here. And it is, simply, amazing. The fascist high officers of the four armed corps had risen up against the Popular Unity government, and only 40 men resisted for seven hours against the weight of the artillery, tank, planes and fascist infantry. Few times in history has such a page of heroism been written.

The president was not only courageous and firm in keeping his word that if need be he would die in defense of the people's cause, but he grew in the critical hour to incredible heights. His fortitude, serenity, dynamism, leadership and heroism were invaluable. Never in this hemisphere has any other president taken part in such a dramatic feat. Unarmed ideas have often been crushed by brute force. Now it can be said that never had brute force come up against such resistance, carried out in the military field, by a man of ideas, whose weapons were always the spoken and written word.

Salvador Allende showed more dignity, honor, courage and heroism than all the fascist military men put together. His incomparable actions sank Pinochet and Pinochet's accomplishes into ignominy forever...

The fascists have tried to hide the extraordinary behavior of President Allende from the people of Chile and the world. They have tried to push Allende's suicide as the "real" version of events. Even if Allende, seriously wounded, had shot himself so as not to fall prisoner to the enemy, it would not have damaged his integrity. It would have been an act of extraordinary courage.

After President Allende's death, they have tried to muddy his name in a low, ignoble, vile attack.

But what can you expect of fascists? They made a big thing of the rifle Allende fought with, the automatic rifle we had given him, using it for their despicable, ridiculous propaganda. But facts have shown that there could have been no better gift for President Allende than that rifle, used in defending the Popular Unity government!

Our premonition in giving the president that rifle was correct. No rifle has ever before been used by such an heroic, constitutional and legitimate president! No rifle has better defended the cause of the poor, the cause of the Chilean workers and farmers! If every worker and every farmer had a rifle like it in their hands, there would never have been a fascist coup!

That is the great lesson which revolutionaries should draw from the events in Chile.

A few days ago, they published a letter we sent President Allende at the end of July. But the fascists are dirty, and many parts of the letter were suppressed. This is the full text:

Havana, July 29, 1973

Dear Salvador,
Using the pretext of discussing with you matters related to the conference on nonaligned nations, Carlos and Manuel Piñeiro are coming to see you. Their objective is to get from you information on the situation, and to offer, as always, our willingness to cooperate in the face of the difficulties and dangers that block and threaten the process.

Their stay will be brief, because they have many obligations pending here, but we decided on the trip even though it involved sacrificing their work.

I see that you are now involved in the delicate matter of dialogue with the Christian Democrats, in the midst of serious events like the brutal murder of your naval aide-de-camp and the new strike of truck owners. I imagine that tensions must be high and that you want to gain time to improve the balance of power in case fighting breaks out and, if possible, find a way to continue the revolutionary process without civil strife, avoiding any historic responsibility for what may happen. Those are praiseworthy objectives. But if the other side, whose real objectives we are not able to judge from here, continues to carry out their perfidious and irresponsible policy, demanding a price which it is impossible for Popular Unity and the revolution to pay – which is quite likely – don't ever forget the extraordinary strength of the Chilean working class and the firm support it has always given you in difficult moments. In response to your call when the revolution is in danger, it can block those who are organizing a coup, maintain the support of the fence-sitters, impose its conditions and decide the fate of Chile once and for all if the need arises. The enemy must realize that the Chilean working class is on the alert and ready to go into action. Its power and fighting spirit can tilt the scales in Santiago in your favor, even though other circumstances may be unfavorable.

Your determination to defend firmly and honorably the process, even at the cost of your life – something everyone knows you are capable of doing – will drag all the forces that are able to fight and all the worthy women and men of Chile into the struggle along with you. Your courage, cool-headedness and audacity in this historic hour of your homeland, and, above all, your firm, resolute and heroic leadership is the vital element in the situation.

Let Carlos and Manuel know how your loyal Cuban friends can be of service.

I reiterate the affection and limitless confidence of our people. Fraternally,

Fidel Castro

All attempts to present this letter as evidence of Cuba's interference in the internal affairs of Chile is absurd and ridiculous. This letter was a message of solidarity, friendship and inspiration that our people gave a president who was harassed by imperialism, reaction and fascism.

Looking at things in such a way, then the universal condemnation of the coup by scores of statespeople, other public figures and many, many organizations; the condemnation of the massacres and other crimes, would also constitute interference in the internal affairs of Chile.

The problems of the anti-imperialist struggle, which affect the revolutionary movement and humankind, also affect and interest revolutionary and progressive peoples all over the world!

For Chile, as is the case for Vietnam, we are not only willing to give part of our sugar rations, we are willing to give our very blood!

When Chile became independent, people from other parts of the hemisphere didn't limit themselves to sending letters, they went to fight alongside the Chileans for the independence of that country.

On September 11, the fascists attacked the Presidential Palace and ruthlessly bombed President Allende's residence, where his family was. It is very lucky that his wife wasn't also killed there. Allende's relatives have told us about their anguish on that day and the following days, when the Chilean people were not told of Allende's death until more than 24 hours after it had happened. The funeral was held in the strictest secrecy. In various ways, his wife and one sister were located. They were taken to a military airport in Santiago, where they boarded a military transport plane and flew to Valparaíso. From there – in the midst of an extraordinary display of forces – they went to the city cemetery, where the Allende family plot is located. The casket was covered by an army blanket, and they never opened it. They never let the relatives view the body of President Allende. Why? What were they trying to hide? They were clearly afraid of exposing themselves. They were evidently trying to conceal the fact that Allende's body had more than 10 bullets in it and that he had been fired on even after death.

The fascists – as you know – also took out their fire on the Cubans, on our embassy. At about noon, the fascists attacked our embassy for the first time. They attacked the second time at midnight. Both attacks were resolutely repelled. We are proud of this! They are aware of the loyalty of the Cuban Revolution, the solidarity of the revolution with the Latin American revolutionary process and this frightens them.

After those attacks, the fascists tried to intimidate our diplomatic representatives. They threatened to use tanks, cannons and planes; but our diplomats repeatedly told the generals and other goons: "We will defend the embassy, which is Cuban territory, to the last person." The fascists knew they would have to kill every last Cuban in our embassy. In the early hours of September 12, they fired sporadically, but the final attack never came off, and our diplomats returned to Cuba once diplomatic relations were broken…

Those events will become more important than they seem to be now, because the fascists are using violence and force in order to impose terror, and there is only one solution for this, only one: having no fear of the fascists!

The exemplary conduct of President Allende morally destroyed fascism in Chile. They underestimated Allende, they were convinced he would get on a plane and give in to force. The fascists were given extraordinary lessons that day, lessons which serve as an indication of the resistance they will be running into, which indicate what is to be expected when people refuse to let themselves be oppressed any longer, when people refuse to let themselves be intimidated, when men and women are willing to die...

Chilean military men have been educated in the concepts of geopolitics, vital spaces, and territorial expansion that are utterly Nazi in nature. Yet not all Chilean officers are fascists. Generals Prats, Pickering, and Sepulveda Esqueda all made great efforts to keep the military institutions loyal to the constitutional government and within the law. Of course, they were forced out of their positions by the fascist majority of Chilean officers and this, unfortunately, opened the way to fascism.

We have also received reports that an officer of the *Carabineros* went to the palace in the midst of the battle and joined President Allende's bodyguards in the fight against the fascists. We must mention these things. The class makeup of the officers of the Chilean armed forces is reactionary, they have seen to it that their officers come from the middle and upper classes – young men of the most downtrodden sectors cannot become officers. Although most of the officers are fascists and have been educated in fascist methods, we are sure that there will be officers who will realize the shameful and criminal role that the fascist leaders are making the Chilean armed forces play and, when the time comes, they will join the people in their struggle against fascism!

September 13, 1973

The new military government names Augusto Pinochet as president, dissolves Congress, and goes on to end all democratic institutions... Pinochet abolishes elections, makes strikes and unions illegal, and imposes strict censorship of books, the press and school curriculums.

The coup has sealed the fate of the Chilean armed forces. They completely exposed themselves. The nature of their "apolitical" stance and their "institutionalism" became clear. Those positions were maintained as long as the interests of the ruling classes were not threatened. But when those interests were threatened, they dropped this alleged apolitical and institutional posture and lined up with the reactionaries and exploiters against the people.

A deep and insurmountable gap now divides the best of the Chilean people – workers, farmers and militant young people – from the Chilean armed forces! That gap is a sea of blood of the workers, farmers, students and murdered revolutionaries, assassinated and massacred by the fascist hordes!

The insurmountable gap made by the blood of Salvador Allende and the men who died together with him that day stands between the fascist armed forces and the Chilean people!

We must say so without fear! Because the people will have to confront fascism – and they will confront fascism!

The military junta is fascist in its ideas and its acts: the mass murder of workers, bombing of universities, burning of books, the concentration camps, and the terrible acts of terrorism against the masses. Dispatches tell of the banning of political parties, the dissolving of trade unions, and crimes and abuses of all kinds. The fascists murder, and when they search communities, universities and the homes of revolutionaries, they plunder ruthlessly and steal everything they can, acting like bloodthirsty and money-hungry bandits... These things: murdering workers, banning parties, burning books, violating international laws, attacking embassies and defenseless ships, and establishing concentration camps are clear examples of fascism in action.

But 40 years have passed since the 1930s, and this is no longer the era in which Hitler and Mussolini stalked the world. There is now a universal awareness which is much more far-reaching. Humankind has advanced and is more progressive; it resolutely condemns these criminal deeds.

The only ones who believe we are living in the 1930s are those stupid, ignorant cretins, the Chilean military goons who carried out the coup d'état.

When we were in Chile, we could see the upsurge of a fascist spirit in the face of the revolutionary movement in the heart of Chilean society. When we left, on December 2, 1971, we told the Chilean people:

> We have learned something. We have witnessed the verification of another law of history – we have seen fascism in action. We have been able to verify a contemporary principle: the desperation of the reactionaries, the desperation of the exploiters today tends toward the most brutal, most savage forms of violence and reaction.
>
> You are all familiar with the story of fascism in the many countries that are the cradle of that movement. You are all familiar with how the privileged, exploiting class destroy the institutions they created – the very institutions they created to maintain their class domination: the laws, the constitution and the parliament – once these institutions are no longer of any use to them.
>
> What do the exploiters do when their own institutions no longer guarantee their domination? How do they react when the mechanisms historically depended upon to maintain their domination fail them? They simply go ahead and destroy them. Nothing is more anticonstitutional, illegal, antiparliamentary, repressive or criminal than fascism.
>
> Fascism, in its violence, wipes out everything. It attacks, closes and crushes the universities. It attacks, represses and persecutes the intellectuals. It attacks political parties and trade unions. It attacks all mass organizations and cultural organizations. There is nothing as violent, as reactionary, as illegal as fascism.

Those things we said then are happening, unfortunately, now in Chile.

Imperialism continues to deny its complicity in and responsibility for the fascist coup. Imperialism is an economic, social, political and cultural system directed at oppressing the peoples. In Latin America, imperialism has tried to prevent the peoples' movements from taking power. In Chile, it was plotting even before the victory of Popular Unity, mobilizing millions of dollars and giving them to the bourgeois parties in order to crush Popular Unity. It won several elections through bribery and the large-scale use of funding, lies, terror campaigns and slander.

Imperialism tried to corrupt the Chilean people. The monopolies tried to corrupt the workers in their mines: as a result of the high price of copper and the monopolies' huge profits, the miners' wages were much higher than those of other Chilean workers.

While preventing Chile from obtaining any loans in the economic field, the Pentagon maintained magnificent relations with the Chilean armed forces. Many of the officers of the Chilean armed forces were educated in imperialist academies. The Chilean government was denied all loans, but Mr. Nixon approved a $10 million loan to the Chilean armed forces for use in purchasing arms just a few weeks before the coup.

Imperialism, playing a shameful game, was driving a wedge between the government and the armed forces, blocking the former and aiding the latter.

Imperialism created the Organization of American States, the Inter-American Defense Board, and the Joint Naval Manuevres Organization. Imperialism created these institutions to plot and carry out counterrevolution in this hemisphere.

The Popular Unity government was not even able to block or forbid the Chilean Navy from participating in joint manuevres with the U.S. Navy.

On September 11, the day of the coup, U.S. warships were positioned just outside Valparaíso. Manuevres by the Chilean and Yankee fleets were to get under way that day. The ships of the both fleets apparently sailed out to sea – and a few hours later returned to Valparaíso to lead the uprising.

In fact, the coup d'état had been in preparation for several days.

When the history of these events is written, the responsibility of [former President] Frei and his rightist clique of the Christian Democratic leadership must be emphasized, as must the responsibility of the reactionary press, the National Party, the judiciary and the parliament for the events which have taken place in Chile, because they will have to settle accounts with the Chilean people.

We revolutionaries must draw our own conclusions from these events. Imperialism is on the move, and it is waging a strategic offensive in Latin America: first the coup d'état in Bolivia, then in Uruguay, and now in Chile.

Ten years ago, the bourgeoisie and imperialism defended themselves with other means: parliaments and bourgeois constitutions. Uruguay and Chile were considered models of legalistic, constitutionalist countries. Yet it was the bourgeoisie and imperialism themselves that rode roughshod over the constitutions and bourgeois democratic systems in Uruguay and Chile, countries which – together with Brazil – now constitute the group of reactionary countries at the service of imperialism in South America…

The Chilean example teaches us a lesson. It is impossible to make the revolution with the people alone: arms are also necessary! That arms alone will not make a revolution: people are also necessary!

We hope this gives our people a better idea about the general situation in this hemisphere.

Some news agencies have enthusiastically applauded the Chilean military coup, also saying that the growing tendency toward establishing diplomatic relations with Cuba will be interrupted…

What grieves us in the case of Chile is not that a country has broken relations with us. These events in Chile hurt us because of the blow dealt to the Chilean people and because of the long and bloody struggle they will have to wage… As far as our relations with the Chilean people are concerned, we have no doubt that the Chilean people will fight fascism. We know the people of Chile. We have been among their workers, farmers and students, and we will never forget the spirit of the Chilean people: their enthusiasm, patriotism and revolutionary fervor, their attitudes. We could not forget the workers or the farmers, from Magallanes to the miners of the north; the coal miners, the industrial workers, the Chilean youth, the fighters and the revolutionaries.

We are absolutely certain they will know how to fight fascism. We are absolutely sure that September 11 marked the beginning of a struggle that will end only with the people's victory. It won't be an immediate victory. No one can expect miracles in the Chilean situation. The people have had a severe blow and the parties and organizations will have to recuperate from the fascist assault. Without any doubt, the Chilean revolutionaries will organize themselves to fight fascism without rest.

Chilean revolutionaries now know that there is no alternative other than revolutionary armed struggle.

They tried the electoral way, the peaceful road, and the impe-
rialists and reactionaries changed the rules of the game, trampling
on the constitution, the laws, the parliament, everything, and
there is no way out of that situation. They can only govern Chile
through force, by means of fascist institutions.

The fascists say now they are going to reconstruct the economy.
They do ridiculous things: calling upon the wealthy wives of the
colonels and generals to donate a few jewels to reconstruct the
Chilean economy. Who will believe this fairy tale? We know the
fascists want to develop Chile's capitalist and bourgeois economy
with the labor and blood of the Chilean workers. We know very
well they will not rebuild the Chilean economy with their fancy
ladies' jewels, but with the blood and sweat of Chilean workers.
Imperialism will surely now give the fascists immediate credit
through the World Bank and other institutions, and will arm
Chile to the teeth.

President Allende has given his people the highest, most heroic
example he could offer. It's impossible for each honest and worthy
Chilean not to feel their blood boil with indignation when confronted with the recent events that have taken place in his country
and the example given by President Allende and by those fighters
who fell with him.

The fascists say that peace has reigned in Chile since
September 11. But, just as surely as there was a September 11 as
we in Cuba had a March 10 [military coup led by Fulgencio
Batista], Chile will also have a July 26 [armed insurrection] and a
January 1 [revolution]!

On arriving at the plaza and seeing this huge, impressive
crowd; listening to the national anthems of Chile and Cuba; and
seeing a million people observe absolute silence in memory of
President Allende – during these moments filled with emotion,
deep affection, and respect for the Chilean people, we were
thinking that some day crowds like this will gather in a Chile without exploiters or exploited; a Chile in which the armed forces
and the people are one and the same; a Chile as well-armed as
Cuba; a Chile in which the people are as united as ours; a Chile
as well organized as we are and with a level of political develop-

ment similar to that of the Cuban people today, without any large landowners, henchmen, exploiters, fascists or bourgeois press; with no radio stations or other means of mass communication that aren't in the hands of the people; a Chile without a bourgeois parliament, without a Rio de Janeiro Treaty, without joint manuevres. We are convinced the Chilean people will succeed; we are sure that, just as the Cuban people succeeded, the Chilean people will also succeed because of their revolutionary spirit, their civic attributes, their enthusiasm, their humane qualities and their courage; and, moreover, because ours is a just cause, the cause of the future, the cause of the peoples' liberation; and because progressive forces are growing and developing throughout the world, and imperialism is on the decline.

We saw how imperialism declined in this hemisphere; we started the process. Our nations will surely see the end of imperialism in this part of the world.

Our people will stand by the people of Chile and give them all the help we can in all fields. We've already given a part of our sugar ration to the Chilean people, and we'll give them our hearts, if necessary, to help the Chilean Revolution! We believed in President Allende; we trusted him. Our people did, too. Our people had the fullest confidence in his integrity, his courage and his willingness to defend his post to the death. President Allende did not let the people of Chile and Cuba down. But neither will the Chilean people fail President Allende. The Chilean revolutionaries won't disappoint President Allende. Above all, they will heed his call for close unity to carry forward the liberation struggle.

The Cuban people too, will not fail their loyal friend, their comrade, their brother in the struggle, Salvador Allende. The Chilean people will overthrow fascism!

"If every worker and every farmer had rifle in their hands, there would neve have been a fascist coup!"

–Fidel Castro

Chronology:
Chile 1970-73

James Cockcroft and Jane Canning

1970

March 25 The White House "Committee of 40," headed by National Security Council Director Henry Kissinger and in charge of U.S. plans to prevent Allende's ascendancy to the presidency or, failing that, of destabilizing his regime until a military coup can overthrow him, meets and approves $125,000 for a "spoiling operation" against Allende's Popular Unity coalition.

June Kissinger tells the "Committee of 40" that should Allende win Chile's elections, "I don't see why we need to stand by and watch a country go communist due to the irresponsibility of its own people." The possibility of an Allende victory in Chile is raised at an International Telephone and Telegraph (ITT) board of directors' meeting. John McCone, former CIA director, and, at the time, a consultant to the CIA and a director of ITT, subsequently holds a number of conversations regarding Chile with CIA Director Richard Helms. Helms' 1970 notes prophesy that an economic squeeze on Chile will cause its economy to "scream."

June 27 "Committee of 40" approves $300,000 for additional anti-Allende propaganda operations.

July 16 John McCone arranges for William Broe (CIA) to talk with Harold Geneen (ITT). Broe tells Geneen that CIA cannot disburse ITT funds but promises to advise ITT on how to channel its own funds. ITT later passes $350,000 to the Alessandri campaign (Allende's opponent) through an intermediary.

August 18 U.S. National Security Study Memorandum (NSSM) 97 is reviewed by the Interdepartmental Group, which considers options ranging from efforts to forge amicable relations with Allende to opposition to him.

September 4 Popular Unity candidate Salvador Allende wins 36.3 percent of the vote in the presidential election, defeating National Party candidate Jorge Alessandri (34.9 percent) and Christian Democrat Radomiro Tomic (27.8 percent). Final outcome is dependent on October 24 vote in Congress between Allende and the runner-up, Alessandri. Traditionally, the candidate with a plurality of popular votes wins the congressional runoff.

September 8 and 14 "Committee of 40" approves $250,000 for Ambassador Korry to use to influence the October 24 congressional vote.

September 9 Harold Geneen, ITT's Chief Executive Officer, tells John McCone at an ITT board of directors' meeting in New York that he is prepared to put up as much as $1 million for the purpose of assisting any government plan designed to form a coalition in the Chilean Congress to stop Allende. McCone agrees to communicate this proposal to high Washington officials and meets several days later with Henry Kissinger and Richard Helms.

September 15 President Nixon instructs CIA Director Helms to prevent Allende's accession to office. The CIA is to play a direct role in organizing a military coup d'état. This involvement comes to be known as Track II. Years later, Helms is convicted of perjury for lying to the U.S. Senate about the CIA's foreign and domestic covert activities.

September 16 At an off-the-record White House press briefing, Henry Kissinger warns that the election of Allende would be irreversible and that an Allende-led Chile could become a "contagious example" that "would infect" NATO allies in South America. He also expresses doubt that Chile would experience another free election. (An ex-aide to Kissinger later noted, "Henry thought Allende might lead an anti-U.S. movement in Latin America more effectively than Fidel Castro, because Allende's was a democratic path to power."

September 29 A CIA official, at the instruction of Richard Helms, meets with a representative of ITT. The CIA officer proposes a plan to accelerate economic disorder in Chile. ITT rejects the proposal.

October Following a White House meeting, the CIA contacts Chilean military conspirators; CIA attempts to defuse a plot by retired General Viaux, but still to generate maximum pressure to overthrow Allende by coup; CIA provides tear gas grenades and three submachine guns to conspirators. ITT submits to White House an 18-point plan designed to assure that Allende "does not get through the crucial next six months."

October 9 Constitutional amendments are introduced into Chile's Congress and later passed, in effect, as a condition for ratifying Allende's election as president. The amendments limit government interference in political parties, education, the "free press," and the armed forces. Allende's power to appoint commanding officers is limited, although he is still allowed to promote officers in the armed forces and *Carabineros*. Allende is obligated to preserve the jobs of the previous administration's state functionaries.

October 14 "Committee of 40" approves $60,000 for U.S. Ambassador Korry's proposal to purchase a radio station. The money is never spent.

October 16 A secret "eyes only" CIA headquarters cable to the CIA station chief in Santiago (made public years later) gives an "operational guide" based on Kissinger's review of covert coup plotting. "It is firm and continuing policy that Allende be overthrown by a coup," the cable states.

October 22 After two unsuccessful abduction attempts on October 19 and 20, a third attempt to kidnap Chilean Army Commander-in-Chief General René Schneider results in his being fatally shot, reportedly by right-wing elements angry at his failure to take military action against Allende.

October 24 The Chilean Congress votes 153 to 35 in favor of Allende over Alessandri.

November 3 Allende is formally inaugurated as president of Chile.

November 12 Allende announces he is renewing diplomatic, commercial and cultural relations with Cuba.

November 13 "Committee of 40" approves $25,000 for support of Christian Democratic candidates.

November 19 "Committee of 40" approves $725,000 for a covert action program in Chile. Approval is later superseded by a January 28, 1971, authorization for nearly twice the amount.

December 21 President Allende proposes a constitutional amendment establishing state control of the large mines and authorizing expropriation of all the foreign firms working them. Both he and the Christian Democratic presidential candidate Tomic had campaigned on a platform calling for nationalization of the copper mines.

December 30 President Allende announces he will be submitting a bill to Congress nationalizing private domestic banks "in order to provide more credit for small and medium-sized businesses."

1971

January 5 Chile establishes diplomatic relations with the People's Republic of China.

January 28 "Committee of 40" approves $1,240,000 for the purchase of radio stations and newspapers and to support municipal candidates and other political activities of anti-Allende parties.

February 12 Chile and Cuba sign a $20 million trade agreement.

February 27 The U.S. Defense Department announces it is canceling the planned visit to Chile of the nuclear carrier *Enterprise*, earlier welcomed by Allende. All Chile's political parties denounce the decision as a slight to Chileans.

March 22 "Committee of 40" approves $185,000 additional support for the Christian Democratic Party.

April 4 Allende's Popular Unity coalition garners 49.7 percent of the vote in a four-way field in 280 municipal elections. For the first time in Chilean history, people 18 to 21 years old could vote. Their support contributed to Popular Unity's huge margin of victory. A CIA-funded fascist group, *"Patria y Libertad"* ("Homeland and Liberty"), begins stepping up a campaign of sabotaging factory equipment to hobble the economy.

May 10 "Committee of 40" approves $77,000 for purchase of a press for the Christian Democratic Party newspaper. The press is not obtained and the funds are used to support the paper.

May 20 "Committee of 40" approves $100,000 for emergency aid to the Christian Democratic Party to meet short-term debts.

May 26 "Committee of 40" approves $150,000 for additional aid to Christian Democratic Party to meet debts.

June 30 U.S. State Department announces a $5 million loan for the Chilean armed forces' purchase of military equipment.

July 6 "Committee of 40" approves $150,000 for support of opposition candidates in a Chilean by-election.

July 11 In a joint session of the Chilean Congress, a constitutional amendment is unanimously approved permitting the nationalization of the copper industry, source of three-fourths of Chile's foreign exchange. The amendment provides for compensation to copper companies within 30 years at not less than 3 percent interest. Also nationalized are iron ore, steel and nitrates.

August 11 The Export-Import Bank denies a Chilean request for $21 million in loans and loan guarantees needed to purchase three jets for the national LAN-Chile airline.

September The chiefs of Chile's main foreign corporations – Anaconda Copper, Ford Motor Company, First National City Bank, Bank of America, Ralston Purina and ITT – meet with Secretary of State William Rogers and agree to an economic blockade of Chile. The CIA sets up a "coup team" at the U.S. Embassy in Santiago and pays out millions of dollars to Chilean right-wing groups, newspapers, radio stations, and political figures to accelerate the destabilization campaign.

September 9 "Committee of 40" approves $700,000 for support to the major Santiago newspaper, *El Mercurio*, which goes on to encourage acts of sedition against the Chilean government, including a military coup.

September 10 President Allende approves Chile's participation in a joint naval exercise with the United States and several Latin American nations.

September 28 President Allende announces that "excess profits" of $774 million in the previous 15 years will be deducted from compensation to be paid to nationalized copper companies. Earlier, separate Soviet and French teams of technocrats and economists had revealed several abuses by the foreign copper concerns. The opposition Christian Democratic and National parties announce their support of Allende's compensation policies in mid-October.

September 29 The Chilean government assumes operation of the Chilean telephone company (CHITELCO). ITT had owned 70 percent interest in the company since 1930.

September 29 Nathaniel Davis replaces Edward Korry as U.S. Ambassador to Chile.

November 5 "Committee of 40" approves $815,000 support to opposition parties and to induce a split in the Popular Unity coalition.

November 10 – December 4 Fidel Castro conducts an extensive goodwill tour throughout Chile.

November 30 After a visit to Latin America, White House Director of Communications Herbert G. Klein tells reporters that he and presidential counselor Robert H. Finch had received the "feeling" that the Allende government "won't last long."

December 1 The Christian Democratic and National parties organize the "March of the Empty Pots" by women to protest food shortages and the visit of Fidel Castro to Chile.

December 15 "Committee of 40" approves $160,000 to support two opposition candidates in January 1972 by-elections.

1972

January 19 President Nixon issues a statement warning that, in cases of expropriated U.S. company properties, should compensation not be reasonable then new bilateral economic aid to the expropriating country might be terminated and the United States would withhold its support from loans under consideration in multilateral development banks.

February 29 New York Supreme Court blocks New York bank accounts of Chilean government agencies.

March 21-22 Syndicated columnist Jack Anderson charges that secret ITT documents (later made public) reveal that ITT had dealt regularly with the CIA in efforts to prevent Allende assuming the presidency in 1970 or, failing that, to bring him down afterwards. In October 1970, ITT had submitted to the White House an 18-point plan of economic warfare, subversion and sabotage against Chile, to be directed by a special White House task force and assisted by the CIA, aimed at precipitating economic chaos whereby the Chilean armed forces, "will have to step in and restore order." One ITT option sent to Kissinger was the halting of all loans by international and U.S. private banks. (Actually, neither the Inter-American Development Bank nor the World Bank had granted new credits to Chile since Allende assumed the presidency, even denying emergency relief to victims of the 1971 earthquake.) Anderson also revealed that in exchange for the Nixon administration's assistance in toppling Allende, ITT had offered to contribute several hundred thousand dollars to the Nixon campaign for the 1972 U.S. presidential election.

April 11 "Committee of 40" approves an additional $965,000 for support to *El Mercurio.*

April 24 "Committee of 40" approves $50,000 for an effort to splinter the Popular Unity coalition.

May 12 President Allende submits a constitutional amendment to the Chilean Congress calling for the expropriation of ITT's holdings in the Chilean telephone company.

June 16 "Committee of 40" approves $46,500 to support a candidate in a Chilean by-election.

July 24 Allende attacks the United States for "deliberately restricting" Chile's credits in 1970-72 and for imposing "a virtual economic blockade" on Chile. (In 1972, Kennecott Copper Company had begun orchestrating an embargo against all Chilean copper exports to the rest of the world. Then, in early 1973, copper prices began plummeting in reaction to President Nixon's persuading the U.S. Congress to legislate the release of U.S. copper stockpiles, thereby creating a glut on the world market.)

August 21 Allende declares a state of emergency in Santiago province after violence grows out of a one-day strike by most of the capital's shopkeepers.

September 21 "Committee of 40" approves $24,000 to support an anti-Allende businessmen's organization.

October 10 The Confederation of Truck Owners launches a nationwide strike backed by the opposition parties. This leads to the government's declaration of a state of emergency, not lifted until November 5 when the new military Interior Minister General Carlos Prats negotiates a strike settlement.

October 26 "Committee of 40" approves $1,427,666 to support opposition political parties and private sector organizations in anticipation of March 1973 congressional elections.

November 4 In a speech honoring the second anniversary of the Popular Unity government, Allende defiantly proclaims the start of "the definitive defeat of the fascist threat."

December 4 Speaking before the General Assembly of the United Nations, President Allende charges that Chile has been the "victim of serious aggression" and adds, "we have felt the effects of a large-scale external pressure against us."

December 8 United States announces that in May 1972 it had agreed to extend $10 million in credit to the Chilean armed forces for purchase of a C-130 air force transport and other equipment, possibly tanks, armored personnel carriers and trucks.

1973

January Inflation reaches 200 percent.

February 12 "Committee of 40" approves $200,000 to support opposition political parties in the congressional elections.

March 4 In the congressional elections, Allende's Popular Unity coalition wins 43.4 percent of the vote, a 7 percent increase over its vote in the 1970 presidential race.

March 22 Talks between the United States and Chile on political and financial problems end in an impasse.

May 10 A three-week copper strike continues at El Teniente mine and a state of emergency is declared in that region. The most determined strikers are the executive and management staff.

June 5 Chile suspends its foreign shipments of copper as miners' strikes continue.

June 15 Allende meets with copper strikers, and the majority of unskilled workers vote to accept his offer and return to work.

June 20 Thousands of physicians, teachers and students go on strike to protest Allende's handling of the 63-day copper strike. The workers confederation (CUT) calls a general strike next day in support of the government.

June 21 Gunfire, bombings and fighting erupt as government opponents and supporters clash during the huge CUT pro-government strike. The opposition newspaper, *El Mercurio,* is closed by court order for six days following a government charge that it had incited subversion. The following day an appeals court invalidates the closure order.

June 28 The army announces the crushing of a "barracks revolt" against the commanding officers and the government.

June 29 Rebel tank and armored personnel carriers seize control of the downtown area of Santiago and attack the Defense Ministry and the Presidential Palace before troops loyal to the government surround them and force them to surrender. This is the first military attempt to overthrow an elected Chilean government in 42 years. The abortive coup was led by Colonel Roberto Souper, who reportedly was about to be arrested as the head of the "barracks revolt" uncovered by army officials the day before.

July 2 Copper miners agree to return to work, ending a 76-day strike that cost the government an estimated $60 million and crippled the country's economy.

July 26 Truck owners throughout Chile go on strike, funded by the CIA, once more crippling the economy.

August Christian Democrats hint broadly that they favor a coup and the party's newspaper runs an article claiming the government has been taken over by a "Jewish-communist cell." To assuage big business, Allende approves the eviction of workers from the more than 1,000 workplaces they have occupied. In some factories troops are required to do the job, and some workers are killed.

August 2 The owners of more than 110,000 buses and taxis go on strike.

August 3 At a press conference, Allende charges that 180 acts of terrorism against railroads, highways, bridges, pipelines, schools and hospitals had been committed since the assassination of his naval aide-de-camp a week earlier.

August 7 The navy announces quashing of a servicemen's revolt in Valparaíso.

August 8 Allende announces formation of a new cabinet including the three chiefs of the armed forces and the chief of the *Carabineros*.

August 20 "Committee of 40" approves $1 million to support opposition political parties and private sector organizations.

August 23 General Carlos Prats resigns as Allende's defense minister and army commander, explaining in his letter of resignation that his participation in the cabinet had caused a left-right split in the army and stating that he was forced to resign by a "sector of army officers." General Augusto Pinochet Ugarte is named army commander on August 24. Prats' resignation is interpreted as a severe blow to Allende.

August 27 Chile's shop owners call another antigovernment strike.

September 4 An estimated 750,000 supporters of Allende's government march in the streets of Santiago to celebrate the third anniversary of his election, chanting "Allende, Allende, the people will defend you!" In a radio and television address, Allende tells them to "be alert, very alert, without losing your serenity." The Confederation of Professional Employees begins an indefinite strike.

September 5 The governing Popular Unity Coalition charges the navy with imprisoning and torturing leftist marines. Allende next day disassociates himself from the statement.

September 8 Commenting on a 2-hour gun battle between air force troops and leftist factory workers, former undersecretary of transport Jaime Faivovich declares, "The armed forces are provoking the workers...

the military coup is already underway."

September 11 The Chilean military overthrows the government. Surrounding the Presidential Palace with tanks, armored cars, riflemen, and jet fighter-bombers by air, they issue an ultimatum to Allende to either resign or surrender. Allende refuses to do either and dies during the battle. In the days immediately following the coup, thousands of Chileans are killed or simply "disappear," as the military establishes complete control over the country.

September 13 The new military government names army commander Augusto Pinochet as president, dissolves Congress, and goes on to end all democratic institutions. Pinochet dismantles Allende's programs and installs a wholly free-market economy. He abolishes elections, makes strikes and unions illegal, and imposes strict censorship of books, the press and school curriculums. Entire university departments (such as sociology) are shut down.

September – October The junta declares all Marxist political parties illegal and places all other parties in indefinite recess. Press censorship is established, as are detention facilities for opponents of the new regime. Thousands of casualties are reported, including summary executions and "disappearances." Many years later, mass graves of some of the victims are discovered.

October 15 "Committee of 40" approves $34,000 for an anti-Allende radio station and the travel costs of pro-junta spokesmen.

[This chronology is taken from the "Salvador Allende Reader: Chile's voice of Democracy," edited by James D. Cockroft and Jane Canning, published by Ocean Press, 2000]

"Venceremos, venceremos
Mil cadenas habrá que romper
Venceremos, venceremos
La miseria sabremos vencer"

Quilapayún [Chilean folk group]

Resources

Books

Edward Boorstein, *An Inside View… Allende's Chile,* International
　　Publishers, New York, 1977

Brody & Ratner (eds.), *The Pinochet Papers: The Case of Augusto
　　Pinochet in Spain and Britain,* Kluwer Law International,
　　The Hague, 2000

James D. Cockcroft and Jane Canning (eds.), *Salvador Allende
　　Reader: Chile's Voice of Democracy,* Ocean Press, Melbourne &
　　New York, 2000

Joan Jara, *Victor: An Unfinished Song,* Jonathon Cape, London, 1983

Pablo Neruda, *A Call for the Destruction of Nixon and Praise for the
　　Chilean Revolution,* West End Press, Cambridge, 1980

Walter Lowenfels (ed.), *For Neruda, For Chile: An International
　　Anthology,* Beacon Press, Boston, 1975

Patricia Verdugo, *Chile, Pinochet, and the Caravan of Death,*
　　North-South Center Press, Miami, 2001

Internet

www.gwu.edu/~nsarchiv/NSAEBB.html
www.pir.org/chile.html
www.thirdworldtraveler.com/Blum/Chile_KH.html
www.frif.com/new98/boc.html
www.wsws.org/news
www.hartford-hwp.com/archives
www.geocities.com/socialistparty/chile.html
www.hormantruth.org

Films, Videos

"The Battle of Chile," widely acclaimed two-part documentary film by
　　Patricio Guzman, 1973-1978

"Chile, Obstinate Memory," documentary film by Patricio Guzman, 1997

"Chile: Hasta Cuando," documentary by David Bradbury, 1986

"Missing," feature film directed by Constantin Costa-Gavras, 1982

CDs

Victor Jara, "Vientos del Pueblo," Monitor International Compact Disc, 1993

Inti-Illimani, John Williams and Paco Peña, "Fragments of a Dream," 1999

Quilapayún, "Lo Mejor de Quilapayún en Chile," 1999

Violeta Parra, "Las Ultimas Composiciones," 1994

rebel lives

"I am in the world to change the world."

Käthe Kollwitz

Ocean Press announces a radically new, radically refreshing series, Rebel Lives. These books focus on individuals — some well-known, others not so famous — who have played significant roles in humanity's ongoing fight for a better world. They are strongly representative of race, class and gender, and they call back from history these lives, catapulting them directly into the forefront of our collective memory.

Rebel Lives presents brief biographies of each person along with short, illustrative selections, depicting the life and times of these

"Better to die on your feet than live on your knees."

Emiliano Zapata

women and men, in their own words. The series does not aim to depict the perfect political model, visionary or martyr, but rather to contemplate the examples of these imperfect theorists, activists, rebels and revolutionaries.

Rebel Lives is produced with assistance from activists and researchers from all over the world, creating books to capture the imaginations of activists and young people everywhere. These books are smaller format, inexpensive, accessible and provocative.

Titles in preparation are:

- Rosa Luxemburg
- Sacco & Vanzetti
- Helen Keller
- Albert Einstein
- "Tania" (Tamara Bunke)
- Chris Hani
- Che Guevara
- Nidia Díaz
- Emiliano Zapata
- Haydée Santamaria

"It is possi-
ble they
will smash
us, but
tomorrow
belongs
to the
people!"

–Salvador Allende